A centuries-old craft, using up-to-the-minute materials and techniques, appliqué offers endless exciting possibilities to the creative needlewoman. And don't worry if you've never tried this fascinating craft before – The Complete Book of Appliqué and Patchwork gives the first-timer full, easy-to-follow instructions – what you need and how to go about creating wonderful effects, whether it's for a full-scale scheme for a bedroom, a simple flower to brighten up a plain garment or a cunningly-disguised repair to a child's favourite dungarees! For those who've already discovered the rewards of appliqué there are more advanced techniques you can add to your skills – professional tips on special effects and finishing touches to give your work that extra something.

Patchwork and appliqué go particularly well together and there's a chapter on patchwork that's especially suitable for combining with appliqué.

You can try out your new skills on the thirty projects, complete with designs and instructions, at the end of the book, or experiment and adapt as the fancy takes you. For every project there's a list of what you'll need, a pattern, detailed instructions and a full-colour picture of the finished item. The projects range from ones suitable for beginners to ambitious ones for the advanced needlewoman, and from practical items such as bags to decorative wall hangings.

THE COMPLETE BOOK OF
Appliqué
&
Patchwork

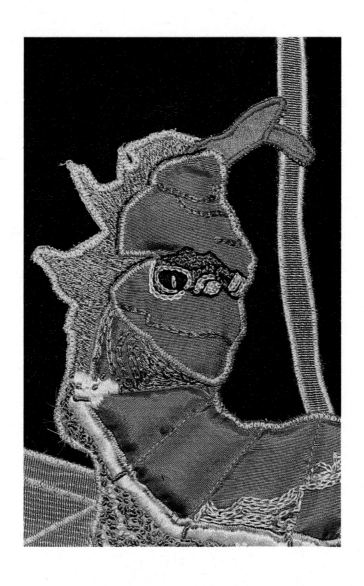

THE COMPLETE BOOK OF
Appliqué
& Patchwork

Lesley Delport

CHARTWELL
BOOKS, INC.

This book was devised and produced by
Multimedia Publications (UK) Ltd

Editor: Valerie Passmore
Production: Karen Bromley
Design: Terry Allen

Published by CHARTWELL BOOKS, INC
A Division of BOOK SALES, INC
110 Enterprise Avenue
Secaucus, New Jersey 07094

ISBN 1 55521 040 6

Typeset by Falcon Graphic Art Limited
Origination by Scan Studios
Printed in Italy by Sagdos

Contents

Introduction

Appliqué, patchwork and *quilting* are complementary forms of needlework. In combination with embroidery they are probably the oldest forms of stitching. Originally they were invented out of necessity but as time passed they were used for decoration. Examples of these crafts have been found dating back to the late ninth century BC.

Early origins

Appliqué, made by stitching fabric patches onto an existing fabric, was devised to repair worn or holed fabrics by covering them with patches. It became more decorative when the patches were cut into shapes and edged with fancy stitches. Appliqué can be traced back to sails on ancient Egyptian Nile boats.

Patchwork, made from scraps of fabric pieced together, was originally invented to make something serviceable from scarce and precious fabric fragments. Patched fabric was extended by joining several lengths of narrow, hand-patched widths together. Patchwork is also depicted in Egyptian murals.

Quilting naturally complemented appliqué and patchwork. For warmth two layers of fabric were stitched together with a soft wadding between them. Decorative forms of quilting came to include stitching in patterns, raised surface work, using cording and trapunto.

Although all three crafts were used for hundreds of years in North Africa, Persia, Syria, Turkestan, India and China, it was not until the eleventh century that Europeans began to use appliqué and patchwork for decorative purposes. The crusaders brought the two crafts back to Europe, having seen the decorative banners and tents of the Saracens, and Europeans began to use both crafts for flags, banners, church vestments, wall hangings, quilts and table cloths. Appliqué and patchwork became visual expressions in needlework.

Quilting in Europe dates back to Roman times when it was used in bed furnishings and as a protective covering for soldiers. Quilted protective clothing was worn by soldiers from the eleventh to the nineteenth century.

In the thirteenth century a decorative form of quilting, known as *trapunto*, was developed in Italy. Its origins were in Persia and India, but the Italian designs were supreme. Two layers of fabric were stitched together by outlining designs with running stitch. The designs were emphasized with stuffing from the back. Another type of quilting, known as *corded quilting*, was also developed.

The Italians and Portuguese made intricate patterns by stitching two layers of fabric together with double lines of running stitch. Cotton cords were then inserted between the lines of stitching to raise the design.

By the fifteenth and sixteenth centuries appliqué and patchwork were being used for all types of household furnishing. Sumptuous fabric and gold thread were very popular. Emblems, coats of arms, lettering, flowers, birds and animals were combined with quilting and embroidery in complex designs. Patchwork also became extremely sophisticated in India at this time.

Another technique of appliqué, called *broderie perse*, developed as well. Designs were cut out of a printed chintz fabric and appliquéd onto a different background fabric with buttonhole stitch.

In the seventeenth century quilting gained in popularity and quilted clothing was extremely fashionable. Bedspreads were embroidered and quilted. New weaves and printed fabrics from the textile industry in the middle of the eighteenth century stimulated their use in patched and appliquéd covers and wall hangings in preference to delicate quilting and embroidery patterns.

Interest in appliqué, patchwork and quilting waned in Europe in the nineteenth century except for a brief period when *gathered patchwork*, a combination of patchwork and quilting, was popular. Patches were stitched together, stuffed and quilted, and these stuffed and quilted patches were joined to make bedcovers.

In North America quilting, patchwork and appliqué flourished between 1775 and 1885. The techniques were taken to America by the early Dutch and English settlers and eventually became a traditional American folk art. Times were extremely hard for the pioneers and supplies were limited; these crafts thrived out of sheer necessity. Social gatherings were arranged for the purpose of quilting. At first the patchwork, appliqué and quilting were done without designs and using simple fabric. As time passed different types of appliqué and patchwork designs developed and were given names such as log cabin, bear's paw, cathedral window, rose of Sharon and many more. Quilts were made for many occasions; friendship quilts were celebrations of friendship with each block designed and signed by a different person; freedom quilts were given to young men when they turned twenty-one; and of course wedding quilts were made for brides.

In the nineteenth century the Industrial Revolution took its toll on handmade crafts, and it was not until the middle of this century that the desire to be creative with these crafts re-emerged. Today there is an exciting resurgence of the old crafts including those using fabrics.

Page 7 *This detail of an old man from a composition called 'Fireplace Family' shows a wonderful choice of materials. The spectacles on the table are embroidered in backstitch with one strand of metallic thread.*

Left *Trapunto quilted cushions: this is a hand-quilting technique where the 3-D shapes are achieved by stuffing the quilted images from the back, as described on page 50*

Right *The shapes of the buildings are first silk-screened onto T-shirt fabric. Double vilene appliqués are superimposed over parts of the design, a technique described on pages 36–39. An illusion of lights in the windows is achieved by delicate beading with bugle beads.*

Below *The Bacchanalian figure stepping into the vat of grapes is machine appliqué embellished with hand and machine embroidery. The vine leaves form an excellent frame around the central landscape.*

Left *This portrait is a computer print-out with fabric appliqué overlay and detailed hand and machine embroidery in shades of grey.*

Right *Metallic thread embroidery and machine appliqué give an illusion of comfortable seats in a vintage car.*

Below *A student deep in concentration while creating her appliqué.*

Bottom right *The detail in this piece of appliqué is marvellous. The Persian carpet is two shades of velvet, machine-embroidered and finished with a hand-made fringe.*

Appliqué Basics

'Arabian nights': this is a hand-bound book with an embroidered figure inspired by one of the characters in the book.

Appliqué comes from the French word 'appliquer,' to put or lay on. It is a stimulating and exciting technique of art in fabric which consists of cutting out fabric shapes and stitching them to a background. Appliqué can range from simple design to fine art and can be decorative or functional or both. Use will determine the choice of fabric, thread, design, colour and stitching.

Although appliqué is essentially two-dimensional, the textures, shapes and stitches used can give it a tactile quality – a third dimension.

Patchwork, by comparison, consists of joining pieces of fabric together, usually in a geometric design. It will be discussed in subsequent chapters. The first four chapters deal entirely with appliqué. Do remember, however, that appliqué and patchwork work extremely well together.

The following list indicates some of the articles that can be embellished with appliqué. It may stimulate the reader to think of others.

Bags
Bedspreads
Belts
Book covers
Clothing – jackets, skirts, dungarees, T-shirts, dresses
Covers – for kitchen appliances, sewing machine, etc.
Curtains
Cushions
Lampshades
Linens – monograms are fun
Mobiles
Pictures
Pillows
Place mats
Quilts
Rugs
Towels
Sculptures
Table cloths
Wall hangings
Window blinds

Selecting and preparing fabrics

Fabric choice will depend in part on how the appliquéd article will be used. Will it be washed? Is it expected to stand up to wear and tear? Fabric choice will also be governed by the appliqué technique you intend to use (hand or machine appliqué). Early appliqué artists had a small choice of textiles including cotton, linen, wool and silk. Today there is a treasure trove of fabrics to choose from. Selecting is difficult, but the function and appliqué technique will help limit the possibilities. Start collecting scraps and soon you will have a marvellous pot-pourri to choose from.

Left *Lesson in action: the author helping a student with a complicated design.*

Right *This detail of vine leaves shows a brilliant choice of fabric ranging from soft, plush velvet to subtle, lightly patterned cotton.*

Fabric suggestions for hand appliqué

The best fabrics to use are light or medium weight, easy to fold and closely woven. Some cotton fabrics with these characteristics are gingham, lawn, chintz and denim. Lightweight woollens are also suitable. Thick or open weave fabrics can be difficult to fold over at the edges. This is only a guide; any fabric can be used depending on the experience and manual dexterity of the appliqué artist. Some synthetic fabrics are pleasant to work with, but generally natural fibres are preferable. The most important item in appliqué is iron-on vilene (a bonded, non-woven interfacing). It stabilizes fabrics, even those which are inclined to unravel or stretch.

Fabric suggestions for machine appliqué

Machine appliqué allows a far greater choice of fabric, ranging from silk organza, which is extremely fine, to heavyweight fabrics with variegated textures such as corduroy, suede, leather, velvet and hessian. Use a very sharp, fine needle for closely woven fabric and a leather needle for very thick leather.

For garments and soft furnishing it is advisable to use fabrics of the same weight and durability. They should also be colourfast and pre-shrunk if they are going to be washed. For pictures or wall hangings, your choice is infinite. Mix patterns and plains, use subtle or subdued colours, vibrating primary colours or seductive texture.

Left *Frayed hessian, lace and embroidered flowers are used to create this scarecrow.*

Right *The fish have been double-vilened and heavily embroidered. The shapes have been laid out ready to be stitched in place on a sheer background in an interesting composition.*

Below *'Pink bubble': the choice of fabrics is wonderfully appropriate and piped bias binding has given an interesting dimension to the bathing caps.*

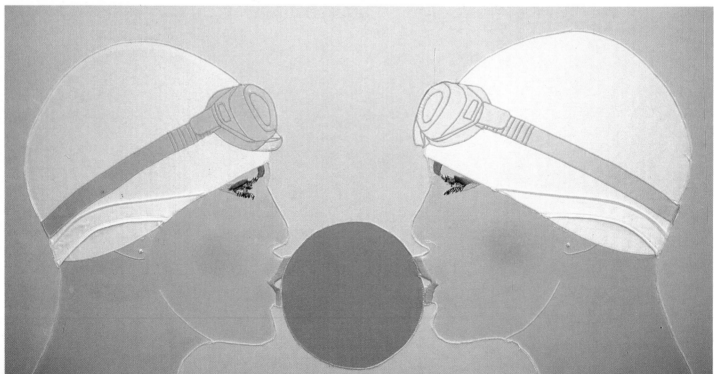

Planning and designing

The first step in appliqué is to plan the design. There are three elements in design: line, form and composition. The following tabulation will help you understand these elements and how they can be combined to create a design.

Line

Line is the basis of form and composition. Different types of lines convey different feelings:

masculine strength

lilt of controlled curve

freedom of a flowing line

Line has direction and direction also conveys feeling:

Horizontal – A feeling of relaxation and informality (modern)

Vertical – A soaring effect (Gothic)

Diagonal – Weak unless supported by opposing diagonals

Straight lines used in opposition – Strong and classic

Controlled curves – Gay and romantic

Free-form curves – Reflect nature (Oriental)

Form

Lines establish shape and form.

static shapes

shapes with movement

Composition

Composition is the grouping of different lines and forms to achieve a unified whole.

The elements of composition are harmony, rhythm, emphasis, scale, proportion and balance.

Harmony: a pleasing and orderly arrangement of parts to create consistency of mood, line and colour.

Rhythm: surface pattern as well as the arrangement of objects. Repetition is a simple way of developing rhythm. More subtle is the repetition of an idea.

Graded sizes also create rhythm.

Continuous line has natural rhythm as in fluted columns or border patterns.

Emphasis: the principal feature in a design. It is achieved by the use of converging lines or by contrast in size, colour, masses of light and dark, or plain and patterned surfaces.

Scale: is related to weight and size. Objects and pattern must be scaled to the article they decorate.

Proportion: applies to space relationships. For example, dividing a design in half is not as intriguing as dividing it in unequal parts. A focal point is more interesting if it is off-centre.

Balance: involves poise and equilibrium. There are two types: formal or symmetrical balance and informal or asymmetrical balance. In formal balance the two halves of a composition are exactly the same. In informal and asymmetrical balance, however, the halves are not identical and the eye alone can tell if they balance. The effect is light, gay and exuberant.

This combination of patchwork pieces has been made in harmonizing shades of browns to blend with country cottage furniture.

Colour

Colour can make or break a design. The colour wheel is a good guide, but colour is personal. Complementary colours (opposite colours on the wheel such as red-green, yellow-purple, orange-blue) give a visual vibration.

Primary colours (red, yellow and blue) are dominant because they are the purest colours. Juxtaposed colours (those colours next to each other on the colour wheel, such as blue, green and violet) blend softly together. Tones (colours mixed with grey) and tints (colours mixed with white) give subtle nuances because of their subdued nature. Neutral colours (black, white and grey) work well with almost any colour.

Pattern and texture

Patterned fabrics must be treated with caution. Tiny granny prints have an olde worlde charm while zany patterns give a high-tech vibration. Too many patterned fabrics tend to confuse the eye and blur the images. Geometric patterns (spots, squares and stripes) give optical illusions and can be used advantageously to create movement and a third dimension.

Another way to create a third dimension is to use textured fabrics. High pile fabrics, such as velvets and synthetic fur, are extremely tactile and suitable for exotic clothing and animals. Loose-weave fabric provides both texture and rhythm. Quilting, embroidery and linear stitching help to unify all the parts.

Enlarging a design

To enlarge a design, draw a grid over it. Then draw another grid the size you want the design to be. The second grid should have the same number of squares as the first. The next step is to draw the design on the larger grid. Begin by finding a square on the enlarged grid that corresponds to a square on the original. It may help to number the squares on both grids. Using a pencil, mark the larger square at all the points where the design intersects with it. Continue in this way until you have marked all the squares on the larger grid. Now join all your marks with continuous lines following the shape of the original design.

pattern enlarged on grid

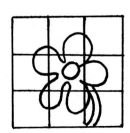

original pattern

The drawing on the grid is your design. If the design is complicated, you may want to trace it and use the tracing as a top reference when assembling the pieces on the background. If the design has many pieces, it helps to number them on the drawing. If a shape is used often, make a template that can be traced around in preparing the pieces. When shapes overlap on the design, draw each pattern piece as though it were uninterrupted. For example, if two petals overlap, mark two full petals on the drawing using a dotted line.

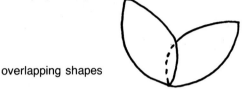

overlapping shapes

Transferring designs

There are many different ways of transferring designs. I advocate iron-on vilene.

Iron-on vilene

A transparent, bonded interfacing, iron-on vilene is ideal for transferring designs because you can place it over the original drawing and trace the shapes in the design onto it. Of the different weights of vilene on sale, buy the lightest, most transparent. These shapes can then be cut out, ironed onto the appliqué fabric and used as a pattern for cutting out the fabric shapes. The vilene also strengthens the shapes and prevents unravelling. The vilene transfer method is slightly different for machine appliqué and hand appliqué.

Machine appliqué

Place your vilene, shiny side up, over the design and trace each shape in the design separately using a medium-soft pencil. Include all the details on each piece. Leave a space of about 12 mm (½ inch) between the shapes. Overlapping shapes must be drawn as if whole or uninterrupted (see illustration above).Where two shapes in the design meet (where two raw edges of fabric will touch), add a 6 mm (¼ inch) seam allowance to one of the pieces on the vilene. This seam allowance will be tucked under the adjacent piece. It should be added to the smaller piece or to the piece where it will not show when the two pieces are in place in the design. Superimposed pieces (those which will lie entirely on top of other pieces in the design) and overlapping pieces need no seam allowances. Once all the vilene pieces have been traced and necessary seam allowances added, cut out the shapes and place them, shiny side down, on the wrong side of the appropriate appliqué fabrics so that the grain of each piece will run in the same direction as the grain in the background fabric when the piece is in position in the completed design. Iron the vilene pieces onto the fabric and cut out the fabric shapes following the edges of the vilene pieces. These vilene-backed shapes are now ready for assembling.

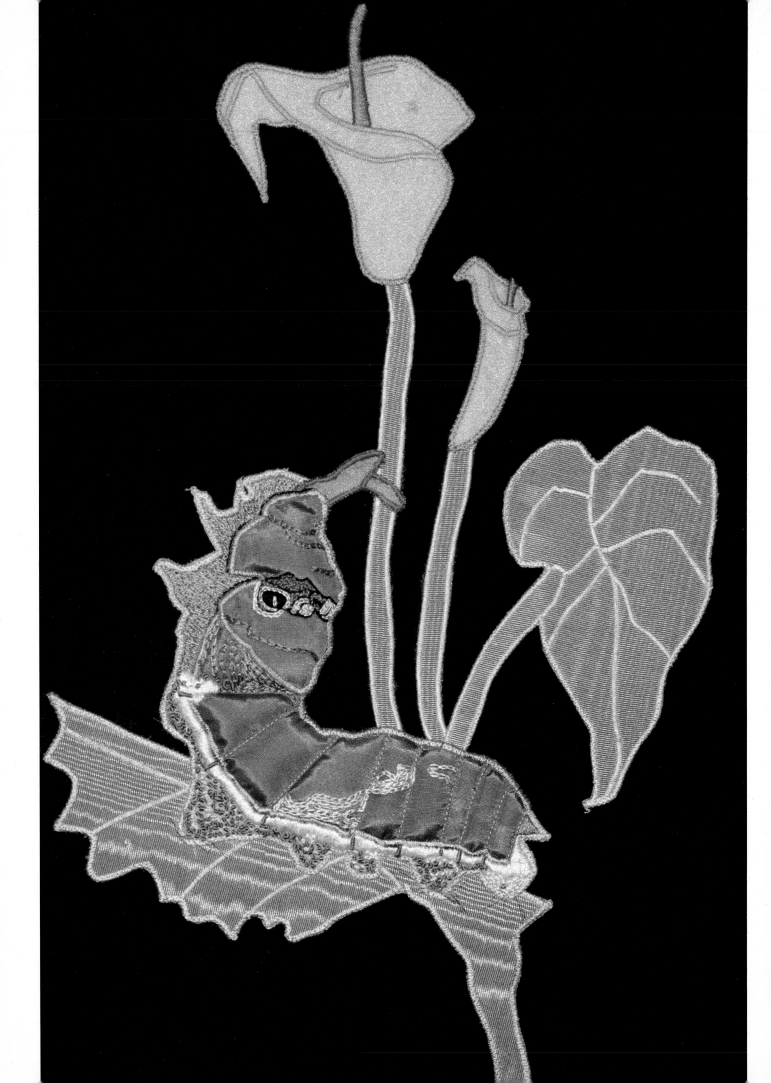

Far left *The stuffed abdomen of the worm gives an interesting third dimension. Transparent nylon gut has been used for the spiky protusions on the abdomen.*

Left *'The Wailing Wall': the small figures are satin-stitched in dominant black embroidery floss. The little tufts of grass in the wall are bullion knots (see page 60).*

Hand appliqué

Place your vilene, shiny side up, over the design. Trace each shape separately using a medium-soft pencil. Overlapping shapes must be drawn as though they were uninterrupted. (See illustration on p19.) It is not necessary to add any seam allowances on the vilene. Cut out the vilene pieces and place them, shiny side down, on the wrong side of the appropriate appliqué fabric, leaving at least 12 mm (½ inch) between each shape to allow for *fabric seam allowance*. Using sharp, pointed scissors, cut out fabric shapes leaving a 6 mm (¼ inch) seam allowance of fabric all round each shape. Now you are ready to assemble.

hand appliqué: seam allowance around **vilene** pieces

original drawing

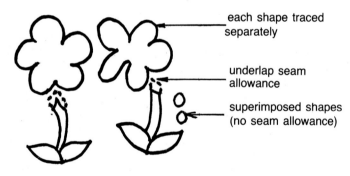

each shape traced separately

underlap seam allowance

superimposed shapes (no seam allowance)

vilene drawing

machine appliqué: vilene pieces with seam allowances included

There are different thicknesses of vilene available. If your appliqué consists of a single layer of fabric, use a fairly thick vilene. If it has multiple layers, for example, shutters, windows and house walls all superimposed, use a finer vilene.

If, after the vilene shapes are ironed onto the fabric, the details on the shape do not show through, hold the fabric up to the light against a window and darken the lines with chalk or coloured dressmaker's pencil. If the fabric is too dark, sheer or textured to take pencilling, tack the details on the vilene side in a contrast thread; a perfect design will appear on the fabric side.

Other methods of transferring designs

Outlines can be traced directly onto the appliqué fabric with a *very light pencil*. This method is recommended when you are using a see-through fabric such as silk organza.

Templates are handy if the design is simple and there is repetition of the shape. Cut them from cardboard, firm paper – or old X-rays make excellent templates. Place them on the appliqué fabric and draw around them.

Special dressmaker's carbon and a tracing wheel can also be used. Place the dressmaker's carbon between the fabric and the pattern. Run the wheel along the lines of the design with enough pressure to transfer the lines onto the fabric.

A hot transfer pencil is good for marking designs on simple garments such as T-shirts where the lines can be covered with fabric paint or beading. A disadvantage of the transfer pencil is that the colour is either too dark or it does not show up on the fabric at all.

A second drawing can be made and cut up into pattern pieces. With appliqué fabric face up, lay out pattern pieces, leaving at least 12 mm (½ inch) between them to allow for seams. Draw around the pieces with a sharp pencil.

Creating your own design

A more informal approach to appliqué is to work directly onto the fabric, forming random shapes and building up the composition as you go along. Texture and stitching (hand or machine embroidery) can be used to give continuity and balance. This type of design is not pre-planned but grows as pieces are attached and worked in.

In creating a design, your choice of motif, colour, texture and hand or machine stitching will depend on the use you intend to make of your work. For example, if you need a quilt but your bedroom is already curtained, your design will be strongly influenced by the curtains. Be guided also by the section on line, form and composition on p.17.

Nature offers a marvellous source of inspiration – floral shapes, landscape (earth, sea and sky) and creatures. The choice is limitless.

Great works of art, children's drawings, wrapping paper and greeting cards can all provide inspiration for appliqué. As in any design, basic art principles governing colour, line, space, shape, repetition and texture will apply.

For details of equipment and supplies needed for appliqué, patchwork and quilting see p112, the introduction to individual projects.

Above *A clever combination of concentric circles and a hexagon frame makes a delightful quilt.*

Below *A strong composition of horizontals and verticals is worked in hessian, leather and suede stitched in hessian and wool.*

Appliqué by Hand

Suitable appliqué stitches   27

*Hand appliquéd, this design is embellished with heavy
embroidery and soft stuffed shapes.*

Whether to hand or machine appliqué is often influenced by your project and by available materials. This chapter covers hand appliqué but do remember that a combination of hand and machine work can give stunning results. Begin your hand appliqué by turning under the seam allowances. This is very simple when you use the vilene transfer technique (see p19). You simply fold the fabric at the edge of the vilene. Stay-stitching is not even required. Tack along the fold around each piece. This will give you a free shape with turned-under edges ready for attaching to your background. Once the seam allowance has been turned under and tacked, you can trim it to neaten. Transparent fabric must have a very small turn-under.

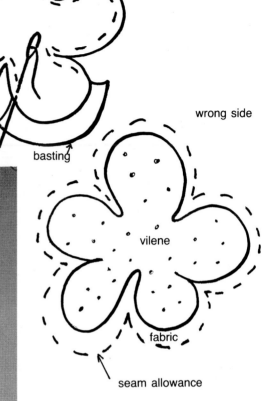

right side

wrong side

basting

vilene

fabric

seam allowance

The small shapes are hemmed by hand onto the background and stuffed when the shape is three-quarters complete. The stuffed appliqué is finished with complementary embroidery.

Another method of tacking is to pin your shapes directly onto the background, turning seam allowances under and basting directly onto the background in one operation. This method is particularly good if the shapes are going to be stuffed. A few appliqué stitches are made and then the stuffing is tucked in place. Be sure not to pucker the background as you proceed.

Curved edges must be clipped and notched to achieve a perfect finish. Clip the convex edges and notch the concave edges.

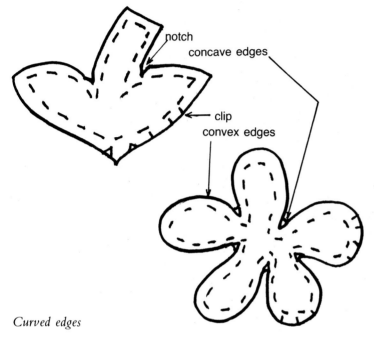

Curved edges

Corners can be turned and folded or mitred to form sharp points (like a parcel).

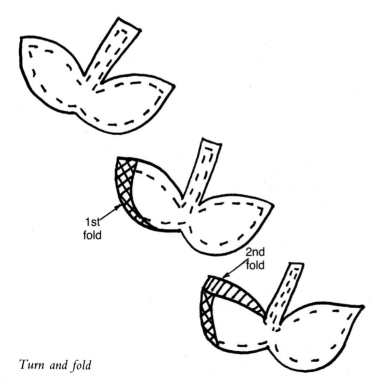

Turn and fold

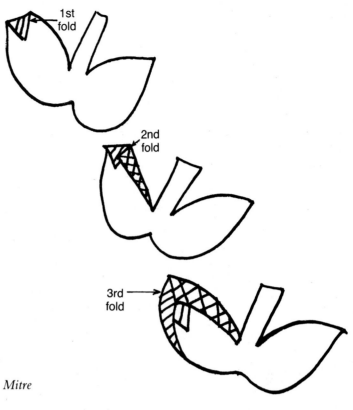

Mitre

If two or more shapes are layered onto the background fabric, do not turn under the seam allowance of the lower shape. Lap the upper shape over the seam allowance of the lower shape and hand appliqué in position; the stitches will hold both shapes together with the raw edges of the lower shape tucked under the top shape.

Suitable appliqué stitches

The next step is to choose from a variety of hand appliqué stitches which are most suitable to attach your appliqué to the background. Tiny whip-stitches, running stitches, blind hem-stitches and back-stitch are all suitable. Backstitch and whip-stitch give a flat edge and are

very secure. In blind hem-stitch, the needle passes along the fold of the fabric and picks up only a few background stitches every 6 mm (¼ inch). This stitch gives a soft, rounded edge and the stitches are almost invisible. The techniques for making these stitches are described below.

Running stitch: Weave the needle in and out just inside the folded edge of the appliqué, taking tiny stitches in the appliqué and background fabric. This stitch is very decorative when worked in embroidery thread.

Whip-stitch: Bring the needle up through the appliqué a tiny distance from the edge and reinsert it into the background at the edge of the appliqué, making a small diagonal stitch. Bring the needle back up again through the background and the appliqué shape. Continue stitching, maintaining the diagonal.

Blind hem-stitch: The stitches must be almost invisible. Bring the needle through the fold of the seam allowance and pick up a few threads of background fabric. Reinsert it through the fold and slide it along the fold about 6 mm (¼ inch). Bring the needle through the fold and pick up a few threads of background fabric. Continue in this manner around the appliqué shape.

Backstitch: This stitch is similar to the straight stitch on the machine. Make a tiny stitch just inside the folded edge of the appliqué. Leave a small space and come up the same distance away as the length of the first stitch. Insert the needle at the end of the first stitch making a small backstitch to meet the first stitch. Bring the needle up a short distance away from the end of the second stitch and continue in this way around the appliqué.

Use matching or contrast thread colour, depending on the desired effect.

An alternative method of hand appliqué is to embroider the shapes to the background. This method helps define the outlines and is both decorative and functional. It is a particularly useful and attractive way to attach stuffed or quilted shapes to the background because they do not fit easily under the foot of the machine. There are many embroidery stitches that are suitable, such as blanket stitch, outline stitch, herring-bone and chain to mention a few. See p58 for information on embroidery stitches. You can also choose from a marvellous range of threads including metallic threads, textured wool and silks. Embroidery details should be added after the shapes have been attached to the background and all tacking stitches removed.

When a shape is very small or intricate, you can cut off the seam allowance and use buttonhole stitches very close together to cover the raw edge and secure the piece to the background at the same time. You can also use tiny whip-stitches close together to give the effect of machine satin-stitch.

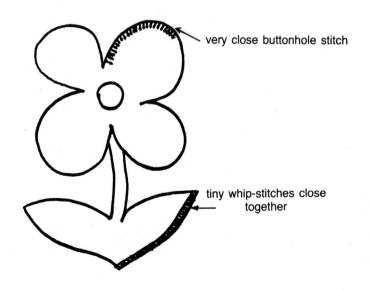

very close buttonhole stitch

tiny whip-stitches close together

Far left One-strand embroidery has been used to create the effect of a wizened old face.

Above *This fish is appliquéd onto charcoal snake-skin. Metallic thread and wool give the illusion of scales and fins.*

Left *The lion's mane is made by fraying the edge of the hessian after hand backstitching a small distance from the edge.*

Right *The wings of this giant crane fly are hand appliquéd with couching in a matching thread.*

If you wish to take advantage of a loose-weave fabric to make a fringed edge around an appliqué shape, hand top-stitch inside the edge to secure the piece and then fray the free edge. Hessian is particularly good for this type of effect.

On an appliqué shape in a sheer fabric, you may want to cut off the seam allowance to prevent it from showing through. In this case, you can define the shape, cover the raw edge and secure the piece, all at the same time, with couching (see p62). This type of work must be protected by glass when framed.

Hand appliqué can also be used to edge shapes before they are attached to the background. Use small blind hem-stitches to secure them to the background. This method is especially useful for shapes that are to be heavily beaded or boldly embroidered because small shapes are easier to handle. Shapes that have been edged with machine satin-stitch can also be attached by hand. Appliqués on stretchable fabrics are best secured this way because the blind hem-stitching will stretch a little with the background fabric. Hand-secured appliqués can also be removed easily for washing.

Machine Appliqué

Note the charming details such as the buttons on the chest of drawers. The quilt is machine-appliquéd patchwork.

Machine appliqué is faster and more durable than hand appliqué. It also offers a host of exciting possibilities using a twin-needle, pin-tucking, tacking and decorative stitch settings for embroidery designs. Machine appliqué is generally done on a zigzag machine, but a straight-stitch machine can be used. (When using a straight-stitch machine, the preparation of the shapes is the same as for hand appliqué with a small turn-under seam allowance all round. To attach the shapes, machine stitch the edges 3 mm (⅛ inch) from the fold.)

In machine appliqué it is necessary to cover the raw edges as well as to secure the shapes. A very close, narrow zigzag setting will give a definite, ridged satin-stitch outline while a slightly wider, more open setting will give a more zigzag-like pattern. Personal taste and the function of the finished piece will be a strong influence. If the zigzag is set too close, stitches will bunch. If using a very close satin-stitch proves difficult, try using a slightly open zigzag which is even and faultless. A fairly narrow width (approximately 2 on most machines) and quite a close zigzag (approximately ½) is suitable for most work. Highly textured fabric might require a wider setting. An experienced appliqué artist can also taper the machine satin-stitch. Start with a fairly wide setting such as 3 and slowly turn the width dial until it is on 0.

An expensive, good quality machine thread will give a really satiny finish to your work. Bobbin tension can be a little tighter than usual; this will pull the top threads through to give a well-rounded top satin-stitch. The colour choice will depend on whether you want to delineate and accent the outline with a contrasting thread or to emphasize colour zones with matching thread. Metallic, silk or any fancy thread takes a certain amount of tension adjustment to prevent the thread snapping or an untidy finish.

Tips to achieve a perfect finish

Guide, do not pull or push the fabric.

See that the needle is very sharp and be sure that it enters the fabric on the raw edge. It is preferable to stitch a little bit in from the edge if following the outline proves difficult. Any stray threads can be trimmed off later.

At a corner leave the needle in the fabric on the outside of the line of stitches. Lift the foot, turn the fabric and start stitching so that the first stitch overlaps the stitch previously made.

Curved shapes can be stay-stitched using a long, straight stitch or an open zigzag. This usually prevents puckering. If there is still a problem with puckering, try a magazine page between the vilene and the sewing machine plate. The magazine is torn away after machining.

When beginning machine appliqué, set the machine on straight stitch, no length (0), no width (0), to knot the threads together underneath. End your work in the same manner when changing thread or completing a shape.

Always machine the details first and then work outwards, trimming excess overlaps as you proceed.

Basic approaches to machine appliqué

Direct application of shapes onto the background

Prepare your iron-on vilene pieces as described on p19. All shapes must be traced separately on the vilene, shiny side upwards. Do not forget to add the 6 mm (¼ inch) seam allowance on one piece where two raw edges of fabric will meet. Remember also to draw overlapping shapes as if they were whole. Superimposed pieces must be traced separately, but no seam allowance is required. Cut out the vilene pieces and place them, shiny side down, onto the wrong side of the fabric so that the straight grain of the appliqué shape runs in the same direction as the straight grain of the background fabric. This should prevent puckering and stretching. Iron the vilene pieces onto the fabric and then cut out the fabric along the outlines of the vilene.

Position each vilene-backed shape on the background according to the design and watch the appliqué grow like a jigsaw puzzle. Single shapes are simple to position on a background. If a design is complex, work systematically from the bottom of the design upwards, tucking any seam allowance in place. It may help to have a tracing of the design which you can place over the fabric assemblage to check your work as you go along. The shapes should be hand tacked in position for perfect preparation, but a stationery glue stick or machine tacking can be used. Tack close to the edge with the same colour thread you will be using for the final stitching. (The machine stitches will cover the tacking so that it does not have to be removed.) Small pieces that are superimposed can be machine stitched to a larger shape before it is tacked in position. Details on the shape can also be stitched before the shape is tacked in position. When all the pieces are in place, machine stitch around the edges using a satin-stitch (narrow zigzag).

Direct appliqué onto the background is suitable for medium to small designs with not too much detail. If the design is too large to pass comfortably through the machine, a different method, called double-vilene technique, is highly recommended.

Grandmother's old rose quilt: each rose has been double-vilened, hand embroidered with french knots and bullion knots, and then attached to the background.

Double vilene technique

The double vilene technique is suitable for large designs or designs on large backgrounds, and is also useful for pieces that are going to be heavily embroidered because small shapes are much easier to handle. Another advantage is that when the design is machined first and then attached to the background, it is slightly raised. In the double vilene technique, the first four steps are the same as for machine appliqué.

1 With your vilene shiny side up, trace the shapes in the design using a soft pencil. Add an under-lap seam allowance where two pieces will meet (see p19).

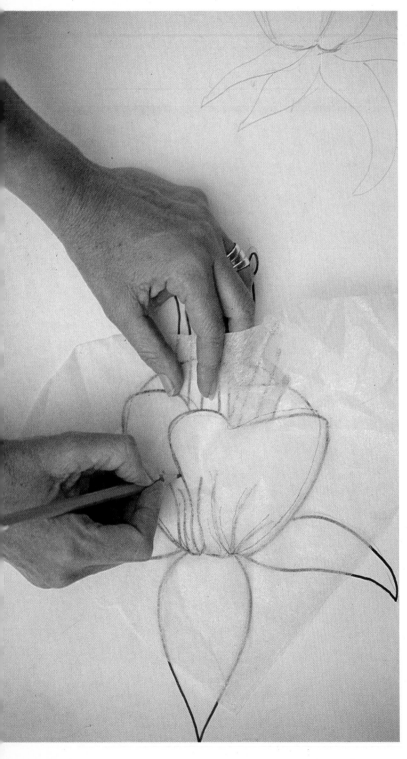

2 Cut out the vilene pieces on your marked outlines.

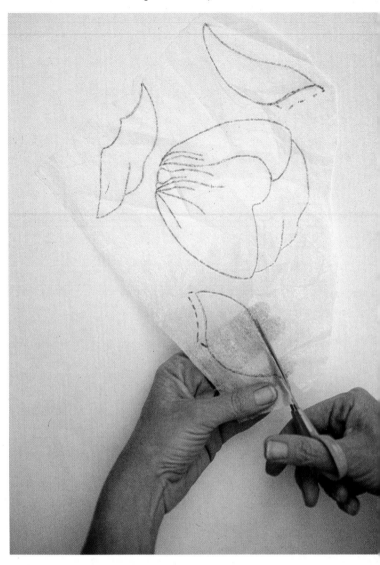

3 Iron the vilene shapes, shiny side down, onto the wrong side of the appliqué fabric.

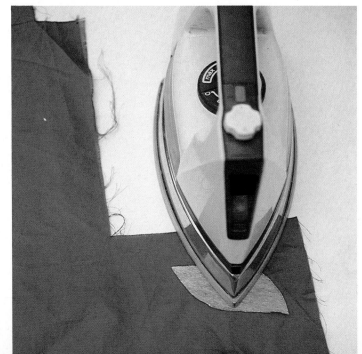

4 Cut out the fabric shapes following the vilene outlines.

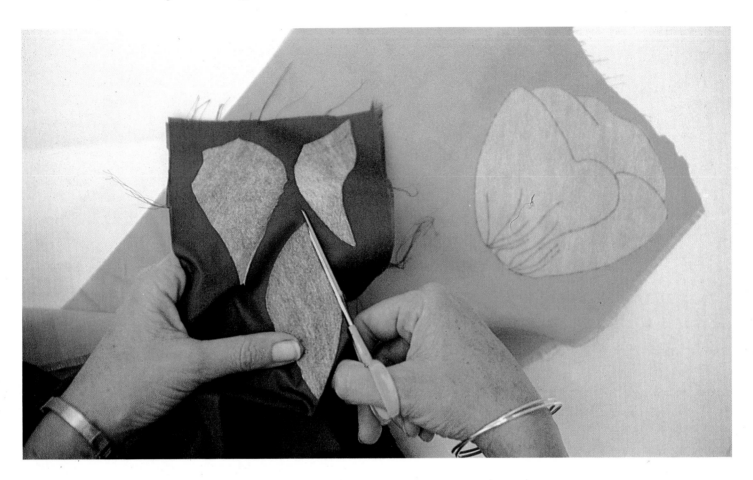

5 Assemble the shapes according to your design on a piece of sew-in vilene interfacing. The vilene should be large enough to protrude all round the edges of the design. Tack the pieces in position.

6 Place the design in the machine and satin-stitch all the raw edges.

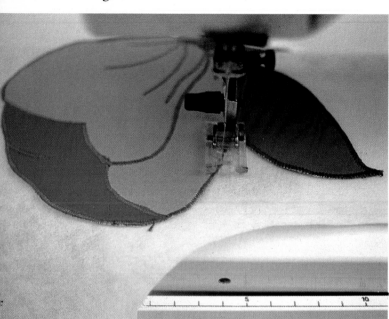

7 Carefully trim away the excess vilene without cutting into the zigzag stitching.

8 Embellish the design as required with machine or hand stitching, beading or quilting.

9 Place the design on the background fabric, glue or tack it in place, and secure it by hand using a small blind hem-stitch or by machine with either a straight stitch just inside the satin-stitched edging or an open zigzag over the satin-stitched edge in the same colour thread.

The double vilene technique is very useful for appliqués on T-shirts and sweaters where the background fabric might stretch. The double vilene appliqué is made first and then hand hemmed onto the garment. The hand hemming gives when the background fabric stretches. The appliqué can also be removed when the garment is washed. I also find this method handy when making quilts. All the shapes can be appliquéd individually, embroidered and then attached when ready for quilting.

The soft sculpture doll is made by stuffing T-shirt material and contouring with a needle and thread. The facial details are hand embroidered.

Special Appliqué Effects

Shadow appliqué

This technique involves the use of transparent materials to give a shadowy effect. There are three different types of shadow appliqué.

A sheer fabric over a heavier fabric

In this type of shadow appliqué, a layer of sheer fabric can be used to cover the appliqué and the background. The stitching is then done through the sheer fabric. A sheer fabric can also be used for one or more shapes in a design. Or it can be used to cover a shape made from a heavier fabric. Either machine or hand stitching can be used.

Hand appliqué

Cut a suitable piece of fabric for the background, for example, a 40 cm (16 inch) square of white cotton suitable for a cushion. Prepare the appliqué pieces without fabric turn-under seam allowances. Working with one piece at a time, position the appliqué pieces on the background, right side up. Continue until all appliqué pieces are glued in place. Cut your sheer fabric the same size as the background. Position the sheer fabric over the appliquéd background. Tack these layers together across the diagonals with a very sharp needle and light contrasting thread. If necessary, tack around each shape. Using a thread slightly darker than the sheer fabric, make tiny running stitches through all layers, just inside the edges of all the appliqué pieces. Add embroidery details at this point. Cut pieces of wadding and lining the same size as the background fabric. Sandwich the wadding between the wrong sides of the lining and the completed top. Tack layers together, from the centre out. Place in quilting or embroidery hoop for quilting. Quilt round each appliqué piece using a tiny running stitch. When all the outlining is complete, the designs will have a shadowy effect with a double line of tiny running stitches around each appliqué shape. At this point, the piece of shadow work can be made up into a cushion or the image can be repeated and the squares made up into a quilt.

Embroidery stitches can be used to attach a sheer fabric to a heavier underneath shape as long as the stitches are very close together or a seam allowance is included.

L. Dalport

seven spotted ladybird.

Far left *As the name suggests, these shadow appliqué cushions are delicate and ideal for bedroom decoration. Tiny running stitches hold the appliqué in place beneath the sheer fabric. Embroidery details provide the finishing touch.*

Left *Brown organza is held in position on the leather using many close french knots, which gives an illusion of a contour and shadow on the ladybird's back.*

Appliqué daisies onto heavier background fabric first. Then place a rectangle of transparent fabric over the stems and satin-stitch around outer raw edges. Finish off by making tiny running stitches along the stems. The transparent fabric gives an illusion of glass in front of the stems

Machine appliqué

Using a tracing of your design or a cardboard template, draw the required shapes onto the transparent fabric. No seam allowance is required. Cut out and position the sheer fabric over the heavier fabric. Satin-stitch the raw edges of both fabrics simultaneously. Using a toning thread, make tiny running stitches just inside the machine satin-stitch edge. Any internal, underneath shadow areas which need accentuating must be delineated with tiny running stitches.

Two sheer fabrics

In this technique a sheer fabric shape is appliquéd on top of a sheer background. This allows a marvellous opportunity to play with colour. For example, if a red sheer is superimposed over a yellow, orange will appear. The effect is soft and delicate, creating an illusion of a shadow. Using two sheer fabrics also permits the use of a hand stitch technique called pin-stitch. The shapes in the top fabric must have a small seam allowance. Appliqué with tiny pin-stitches, pulling the thread tight with each stitch. A line of decorative holes will appear around each shape. Pin-stitch is like a double backstitch alternating with a whip-stitch.

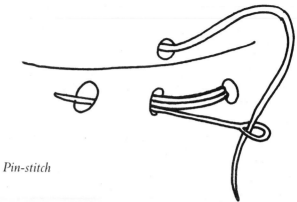

Pin-stitch

Left *The clown's ruff shows an interesting use of two sheer fabrics. The shape is first drawn onto the sheer. It is then cut out and placed over another piece of sheer fabric. The raw edge of the top shape is overlocked with a close zig-zag and the excess underneath sheer is trimmed away.*

Right *The antique lace curtains have been invisibly hemmed to the appliqué windows. The background filters through the fine mesh of the old lace.*

Two sheers can also be used to create a transparent shape. Cut one piece of sheer the exact size of the shape required and place it on top of a larger piece of sheer fabric. Machine appliqué around the top shape. Cut excess background away. The result is a perfectly overlocked transparent shape.

Two sheer fabrics combined with a heavier fabric

A heavier fabric shape can be slipped between two layers of sheer fabric and then top-stitched. This is suitable for free-standing appliqués such as wall panels, screens or table mats.

Reverse appliqué

This difficult technique originated with the Cuna Indians of Panama and Colombia, but it has been adopted by the Western world. Several layers of fabric are tacked together and the top layers are then cut away to reveal the colours beneath. Careful planning is essential.

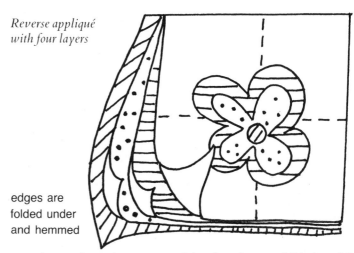

Reverse appliqué with four layers

edges are folded under and hemmed

One large shape is cut out of the first layer of fabric with fine embroidery scissors. The edges are turned back and sewn down with fine, invisible hem-stitches. Within the first shape another shape is cut out of the second layer and the edges are finished. The work continues in this way until the entire design has been worked.

Lace and ribbon appliqué

Old lace and ribbon can be combined with appliqué shapes to add interest to a design.

Ribbon can be attached with a machine straight stitch or a small zigzag stitch or it can be hand hemmed in position. Lace and ribbon also work very well together on their own to create a pattern on the background. They can be successful on scatter cushions, duvet covers and handbags.

Left *Two lines of gathering in multi-coloured ribbon make a charming ruffle for a clown.*

Above *Rows of lace and ribbon on cushions or on the edge of a doll's dress are attached with tiny open zig-zag stitches. This is an excellent way of using up old scraps of ribbon and lace.*

Below *The ribbon basket weave is attached to the background and edged with piped bias binding using blind hemming stitch. The shells are double-vilened, embroidered and attached to the basket with a little stuffing for an added dimension.*

Vertical stripes of ribbon are pinned in position and stitched at the ends. Contrast ribbon is woven horizontally over and under the vertical ribbons creating a basket weave.

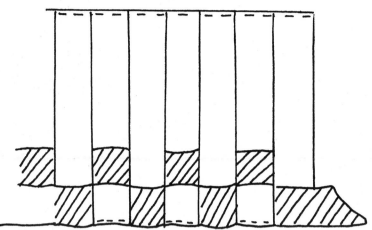

Ribbon basket weave

The third dimension: stuffing, trapunto and quilting

These techniques can all be used individually or in combination to create a diversity of forms in appliqué and patchwork.

Stuffed shapes

Stuffed shapes give a third dimension. Two pieces of fabric are seamed together and stuffed with wadding. This shape can then be quilted or embroidered for added interest and dimension before it is finally attached to the background.

Above *The free-standing petals are made by placing two shapes, right sides together, machining and turning through. Top quilting gives definition to the petals.*

Below *The animals are double fabric, stuffed shapes. They are attached to the background appliqué with hooks and eyes so that their positions can be altered.*

First method

Transfer your shape onto the appliqué fabric. (Use the iron-on vilene technique, a template or a traced pattern.) Allow a 6 mm (¼ inch) seam allowance all round, fold the fabric and cut out two shapes. With right sides together, machine straight stitch the shapes together. Trim the seam allowance, clip the curves and turn through. Now lightly stuff the shape. The opening can be closed by turning the raw edges under and whip-stitching. The opening can also be closed when the shape is positioned on the background and satin-stitched in place.

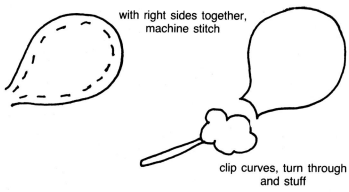

with right sides together, machine stitch

clip curves, turn through and stuff

Second method

Prepare a vilene-backed fabric shape. Cut out a piece of fabric larger than the shape. Place the shape on a larger piece of fabric and machine appliqué around the edges, leaving a small opening for stuffing. Stuff, close opening and cut away excess fabric.

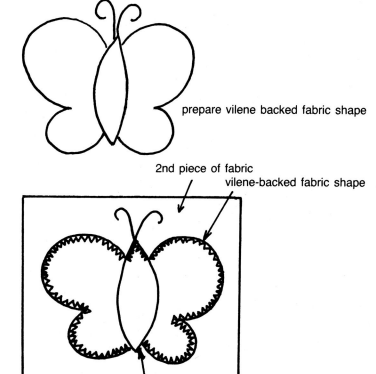

prepare vilene backed fabric shape

2nd piece of fabric
vilene-backed fabric shape

stuff here

You can also stuff shapes during the process of hand appliqué. When the shape is about three quarters of the way attached to the background, push a little wadding between the shape and background with a sharp instrument such as a knitting needle. Do not overstuff or the background will distort. Continue stitching around the shape. These are stuffed shapes but not free-standing.

Material or lace can be gathered and positioned under stuffed shapes for extra interest.

The skirt is made by gathering a double layer of organza and tucking it under softly-padded upper shapes.

Trapunto

Trapunto is high relief worked through the fabric from the back. Proceed with the appliqué as usual using machine satin-stitch. When the stitching is complete, make a small cut in the background fabric behind the shape to be raised. If the weave of the background fabric is loose enough, do not cut but simply push the stuffing between the threads. Gently push the stuffing into the cavity until the required relief is achieved. Close the opening with small whip-stitches. Trapunto can be raised to achieve different levels of relief. Surface details and contours are made by hand on the front of the work with corresponding or contrast thread depending on the desired effect.

tack before hand quilting

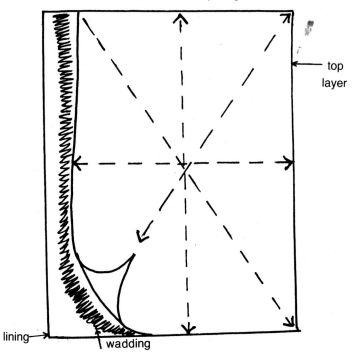

top layer

lining

wadding

Quilting

To go into quilting in depth would require a complete book. But I will cover the basics so that you can use this technique in conjunction with appliqué. There are additional quilting tips and more details in the patchwork section.

Quilting is both functional and decorative; it gives warmth, depth and pattern. The quilting stitches hold the wadding in place and keep it from bunching. They either follow the outlines of shapes in the design or the fabric or they create decorative patterns on the background. Quilting can be done by hand with small running stitches or by machine. Fabric that is going to be quilted must be preshrunk and colour fast. Remember to use compatible fabrics.

Hand quilting

Soft cottons work well for the top layer in quilting. For the stuffing or padding polyester wadding is ideal as it washes well and is light to handle. Number 50 quilting thread is suitable for most quilts and a quilting hoop helps to hold the layers in place while you work.

Sandwich the wadding between the top fabric and the lining and tack the three layers together. Tack from the centre out towards each of the corners.

Patterns can be drawn onto the fabric with chalk, dressmaker's pencil or a light pencil; the lines are then covered with running stitches. If there is a repeat pattern, use a template.

Begin quilting in the centre of the quilt and move outwards. Start with a backstitch to secure the thread and then use tiny running stitches – about 5-9 stitches every 2.5 cm (1 inch). It is very important to keep your stitches even; the length of the stitch and the space between the stitches must be even. Running stitches normally follow the lines of the quilting pattern. Where an appliqué fabric shape requires quilting, the running stitches are usually made 6 mm (¼ inch) inside the fabric outline. If a quilt is made up of many different appliqué designs, it is easier to work on small sections and then join these sections together after they are completed.

Trapunto and quilting combined

Trapunto can be combined with quilting to make a cushion cover or a quilt. Cut a piece of background fabric and a corresponding piece of muslin about 46 cm (18 inch) square. Put them together with the right side of the background fabric on top. Mark the quilting design on the background fabric using an erasable marking pen, a dressmaker's pencil or a very light pencil. Begin by quilting the outlines of the part of the design to be stuffed. Make a small slit in the muslin (or push the weave open) and insert your stuffing into the cavity formed by the outlining stitches. Close the slit. Now cut a piece of wadding and lining the same size as the background fabric. Sandwich the wadding between the top layers and the lining. Tack.

Quilt through all the layers (lining, wadding, muslin and cotton) using tiny running stitches and moving from the trapunto outwards.

Far left *The third dimension of the head is achieved by stuffing the shape from the back – trapunto.*

Centre *This detail shows the many layers required when doing trapunto quilting – top layer, wadding and lining.*

Left *Here we have a combination of trapunto and quilting. The trapunto shapes are made first, and then the background is quilted moving from the centre outwards.*

Corded quilting

Corded quilting is a type of trapunto. Two layers of material are stitched together with parallel lines of running stitches in designs and patterns. Piping cord is then inserted between the parallel lines of stitches with a needle.

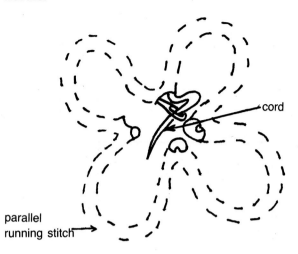

cord

parallel
running stitch →

Machine quilting

Preparation for machine quilting is the same as for hand quilting. Use a strong machine thread and increase the stitch length to about 3½. Often the appliqué design or the background fabric itself will suggest the best quilting pattern. Start machining at a corner and stitch to the opposite corner. Do not change direction until all the quilting lines in that direction have been completed. This is especially important in diamond and block quilting. Sometimes it is easier to quilt an appliqué with just the wadding and top layer, omitting the lining. The lining can be attached at the end with tiny holding stitches or with buttons, tufts or bows through all three layers in a few places and with a border binding. If the design can be broken up into smaller sections, quilt them separately, one at a time. It is easier to feed small quantities of fabric and wadding through the machine, and bunching and puckering can be avoided this way.

Echo quilting

A simple method of quilting appliqué is to echo the lines retaining the shape of the appliqué. No marking is required. Position the foot next to the appliqué and straight stitch all round the designs using the foot space as your guide. Continue quilting until the entire background is patterned.

A 'Little Soft Sculpture'

Trapunto and quilting are relatively low relief. Appliqué can also be used to make free standing shapes or forms in the round that are actually soft sculpture. To make a free standing shape, you will need two pieces of fabric with seam allowances. Gussets, additional side pieces of fabric, will give more rounded forms. The padded shapes can be worked in using a matching colour thread. Start with a small backstitch and pass the needle through the required thickness. Bring the needle out opposite the backstitch.

Take a tiny stitch and return the needle under the padding to just above the backstitch. Pull the thread firmly until the required contour forms. Run as many strands in and out as needed to raise the design. This method of soft sculpting is ideal when creating body contours. Magical soft sculptures are possible if creative imagination is allowed free rein.

Above *This little face is made by wrapping a pink stocking around wadding and creating the face contours with matching thread and bead details.*

Far left *This quilt was drawn onto a large piece of calico. Each shape was made and attached from the base upwards. The shapes were under stuffed and machine quilted to close each area of wadding.*

Left *This design was adapted from a Shabbat songbook. Wonderful rhythm is achieved using echo quilting.*

53

The Finishing Touch

This is a wonderful example of shaded long and short satin stitch, french knots, continuous chain and buttonhole stitch.

Adding embroidery, beadwork, fabric painting and fancy machine embellishments to appliqué is probably the most exciting aspect of the whole creative adventure. These techniques allow the creator to extend stitchery and design in new directions. They are the finishing touches that can transform a piece of appliqué or patchwork from the ordinary to the sublime.

Embroidery

There are many more stitch variations than can be included but the following basic stitches and guidelines should provide a good starting point for any aspiring creator. Embroidery is like painting with a needle and thread – be adventurous and spontaneous and your results should be stunning.

Equipment
Needles
Use the correct needle for the thread and fabric with which you are working. Generally an embroidery needle with an eye large enough to hold the thread and small enough to pass easily through the fabric is the correct choice. Blunt needles are useful for working stitches that pass through other stitches rather than through the fabric, such as woven stitches like basket weave and spider's web.

Crewel needles (sizes 5-10) have sharp points with long oval eyes. Suitable for fine to medium work with stranded threads.

Chenille needles also have sharp points and oval eyes but are bigger than crewel needles. These are useful for heavy threads and fabrics.

Beading needles are very long and thin with a tiny eye which will pass easily through beads.

Leather needles have very sharp, triangular bevelled points which cut easily through leather.

Tapestry needles have large oval eyes and rounded points, ideal for working with wool.

Thimble and scissors
Use a leather or metal thimble. A small pair of sharp pointed scissors is essential.

Fabrics
Any kind of fabric is suitable for decorative stitching. The appliqué and patchwork will provide the ground fabric and can range from silk to leather. Your choice of thread and stitch technique will be governed by the purpose and design of the work. They will help you decide, for example, whether to do surface embroidery or beading or flat or raised work and whether to choose fine or coarse threads.

Threads
It is useful to have a collection of different threads – wool, textured threads, string, crochet cotton, lurex and embroidery thread of all types. Embroidery threads are usually colour-fast and wash well.

Six-stranded cotton is loosely twisted, mercerized thread with a light sheen. It can be separated easily into single strands and used in different multiples. A bullion knot, for example, is most successful using three strands.

Pearl cotton is a non-stranded thread with a sharply-defined twist and shiny finish.

Crewel wool is very fine, firmly twisted 2-ply yarn.

Metallic threads in gold and silver, red, green and blue are also available. These threads usually come in two strands and can be waxed. When using any fine thread which tends to tangle and knot, pull the thread through a block of beeswax, which prevents the thread from separating and knotting.

There are many other embroidery threads in silk, linen and cotton.

Embroidery rings
An embroidery ring supports and keeps taut the ground fabric while the embroidery is being worked. It consists of an outer and inner ring of wood with a screw attachment on the outer ring to adjust the tension.

Enlarging and transferring designs

These methods are almost the same as those used to enlarge and transfer appliqué designs.

Enlarging designs

Draw a grid over the original design. Then, on a separate piece of paper, make the same number of squares on a larger scale. Copy the design, square by square, from the smaller to the larger grid. For more details see p19.

Transferring designs

Often the design for embroidery is already marked on the fabric. However, if it is not marked, there are a number of methods of transferring designs onto the fabric.

Iron-on vilene interfacing: Place the vilene, shiny side down, over the drawing. Trace the design onto the vilene using a soft pencil. Cut out the shape and place it, shiny side down, in position on the wrong side of the appliqué or patchwork. Iron in place and the design is ready to embroider. This vilene transfer gives a lovely raised area of embroidery because it provides an underneath padding to work over.

Tracing paper transfer: Using masking tape, attach your design to a window pane. Place a piece of tracing paper over it and, with a pencil, trace the outlines. Copy the design through onto the reverse side of the tracing paper, place this against your fabric and draw over the design with enough pressure to transfer the design onto the fabric. Hot-transfer pencil can also be marked on the back of the tracing paper and the design ironed onto the ground fabric.

Tacking through tissue paper: Trace the design on tissue paper. Pin the tissue paper design onto the fabric, tack around the outline and then tear the paper away. This technique is excellent for working on dark colours or high-pile fabrics.

Tracing directly from the drawing: This method is used for sheer fabrics such as silk, lawn and organza. Place your fabric over the design and trace over the outlines with a pencil. If you find that lead pencil marks the embroidery thread there are dressmaker's pencils in pink, blue and white as well as fabric pens which either wash out or fade after 24 hours.

Dressmaker's carbon: Trace the design onto tracing paper. Then place the dressmaker's carbon, face down, between the ground fabric and the tracing. Draw over the outlines to transfer the design onto the fabric.

Far left Tiny green beads threaded in groups of three give a raised effect to this leather appliqué.

Left A wealth of finishing touches is being used on this piece of work – lace, twin needle machining, and hand embroidery details.

Useful stitches

Stem-stitch

Work from left to right, keeping the thread to the left of the needle and making small, even stitches. By repeating this stitch you can fill an area. When stem-stitch is used to attach hand appliqué, it is often referred to as outline stitch.

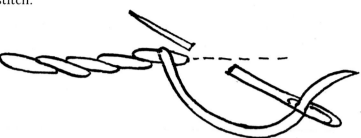

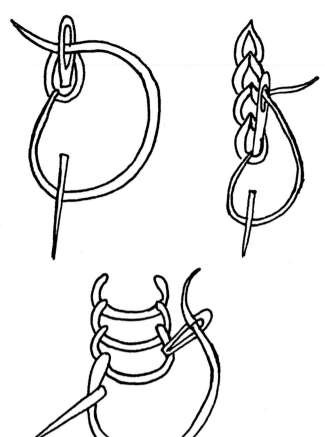

Backstitch

Bring the thread through the fabric and take a small stitch backwards. Then take the needle forwards under the fabric and come out one stitch length ahead ready for the next stitch backwards. Keep all the stitches the same size. Ideal for facial outlines on appliqué.

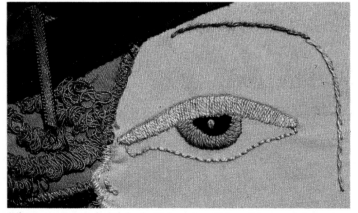

This eye is created with backstitch, satin stitch and long and short stitch.

Detached chain *(lazy daisy)*

Make a single chain-stitch and anchor it with a small straight stitch. Five small, detached chain-stitches arranged like a flower make a daisy – hence the nickname "lazy daisy".

Chain-stitch

Bring the thread through the fabric. Hold the thread to the left making a loop shape. Re-insert the needle at the starting point, bring it out again a short distance away and take it over the loop of thread. Pull through. Repeat the loop inserting the needle exactly where the thread came out, inside the previous loop. Chain-stitch can be used as a filler if it is worked in continuous rows. Always work in the same direction, beginning each new row at the same end. Continuous chain may also be used in a circle.

Raised chain stitch

This is a difficult combination stitch. Make a ladder of parallel stitches approximately 3 mm (⅛ inch) apart. Bring the thread through the fabric at the beginning of the ladder. Pass the thread over and under the first strand. Pull through, keeping the thread taut. With the thread to the left, make a loop by passing the needle downwards under the same strand, to the right of the first stitch, and over the thread of the loop. Do not pull too tightly. Continue making the chains along the ladder. If the bar is wide, several rows of raised chain can be worked. Always start at the top.

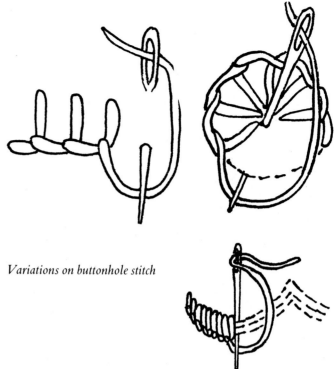

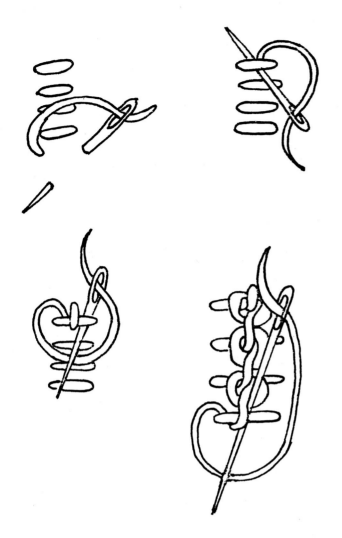

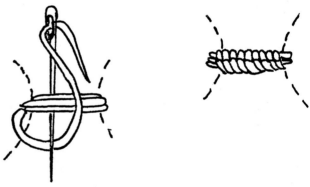

Variations on buttonhole stitch

Buttonhole bars

Take the thread back and forth over a space 2 or 3 times and secure with a small stitch. Buttonhole around the loose strands without picking up the ground fabric.

These crysanthemums are embroidered in raised chain, bullion rosebuds and continuous chain stitches.

French knots

Bring the needle through the fabric. Hold the thread taut with the left hand while wrapping the thread around the needle one, two or three times. Reinsert the needle close to where the thread emerged. French knots can be scattered like little seeds or used to fill an area. They are ideal for the centre of flowers.

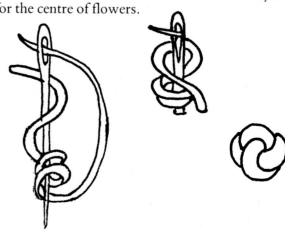

Buttonhole (blanket) stitch

This is an excellent stitch for decorative hand appliqué or patchwork because it is extremely versatile. It can be worked closed or open or radiated to form a circle. It can also be used to create buttonhole bars and scalloped edges. Bring the needle through the fabric. Insert the needle above and to the right of the first stitch, and come out parallel to the bottom of the first stitch with the thread held under the needle. Pull through downwards.

Above *This double vilened shape is detailed with intricate embroidery before being used in a complex design.*

Below *Bullion knot delphiniums and pekinese stitch spidery orange flowers demonstrate the effects of different stitches.*

Bullion knots

The bullion knot is a long, 'sausage-shaped' knot. Bring a small-eyed needle through the fabric. Pick up the fabric the distance required for the bullion knot, but do not pull the needle through. Twist the thread several times round the needle. Holding the coils on the needle with your thumb, pull the thread through and insert the needle at the starting point to anchor the bullion knot. These knots may be worked individually or in rows or in a combination to form a bullion rosebud.

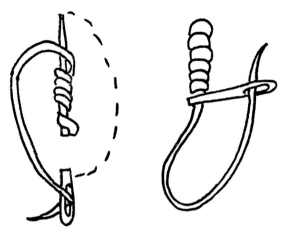

Bullion rosebud

Make a small 6-twist bullion knots. Then make another 8-twist bullion knots each side of the first bullion knot. This size rosebud is ideal for smocking decoration, but the size can be increased by adding successive bullion knots with increasing numbers of twists on each side.

Spider's web

Whipped: Make two crosses creating eight spokes. Bring the needle up in the centre of the spokes and pull through. Using a blunt needle, wrap the thread around the spoke just behind the exit thread, slide the needle under that spoke and the next one. Ie the needle goes back around one and under two spokes until all the spokes are covered.

Work tightly in the centre to accent the whipped spokes, allowing the threads to become slightly looser towards the outer edge. Colour changes can be made. The spokes can be covered completely or the centre may be worked leaving part of the original spokes showing. Any size can be made and tiny spider webs look just like daisies.

Woven: Make a circle of an uneven number of spokes. Beginning in the centre, weave over and under alternate spokes until the circle is filled. This woven spider's web gives a basket weave effect.

A woven spider's web made with an even number of spokes gives a totally different effect, resembling a catherine wheel.

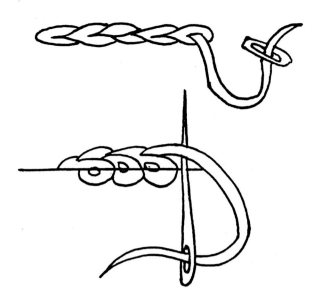

Whipped and woven spider's web stitch

Weaving stitch

This stitch is very effective if you want to create the illusion of a basket weave. Make a series of long stitches, side by side, the width of one thread apart. With a blunt needle, using a contrast thread, weave over and under the threads, starting at the widest part. Push the threads together as each line is worked so that even squares of each colour appear.

Pekinese stitch

This is another decorative weaving stitch. Make a foundation row of backstitch and then, working from the left, weave through the backstitches forming a braid-like effect. You can use the same colour or contrast thread.

Split-stitch

This stitch is made using an even number of strands. Make a single straight stitch. Now bring the needle back up between the strands, piercing through the centre of the stitch from below, dividing the strands exactly in the middle. Repeat forming a neat line of stitches. I find this stitch particularly good for filling in large areas. In order to achieve a smooth finish stagger the splits by making the split a little past or a little short of the split on the previous row.

Satin-stitch

Satin-stitch looks easy but it takes practice to make it perfect. The stitches should fit closely together with very smooth and straight outside edges. The stitches may be straight or slanted. For large areas use long and short satin-stitch for delicate shading.

Long and short stitch

The outline of the shape can be marked with split-stitch, chain or even a small running stitch. Work your first row of long and short satin-stitches, following the outline of the shape. In the following rows, all the stitches will be of equal length, and use a thread which is slightly lighter or darker to give a shaded effect.

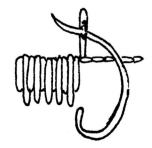 

Romanian stitch

Romanian stitch is a satin-stitch held down with a smaller, slanting stitch in the centre. The stitches can be worked very closely or slightly apart.

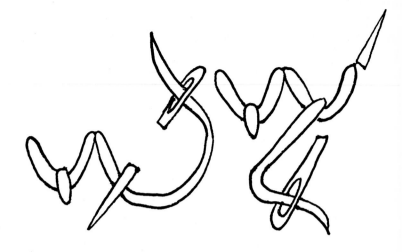

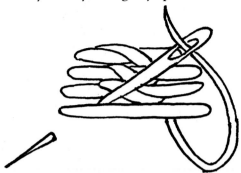

The hair is a superb example of closed Romanian stitch. The face has been embroidered with one strand of embroidery floss and the necklaces and bracelets are a combination of raised chain, pekinese and continuous chain stitches.

Fly-stitch

This stitch is very similar to Romanian except that the 'V' shape is more marked. Make a satin-stitch but come up in the centre of the stitch at a diagonal. Pull through and anchor the stitch with a small tying stitch.

Couching

This technique can be used in linear work or as a solid filling. Threads are laid down on the surface of the fabric and held in place with another thread. Any type of thread may be couched; contrast colours can be used and many different holding stitches are suitable including cross-stitch, herring-bone, straight stitch, fly-stitch and detached chain. When couching in a circle, try and create a rhythm with the holding stitches by controlling the pattern made by the stitches.

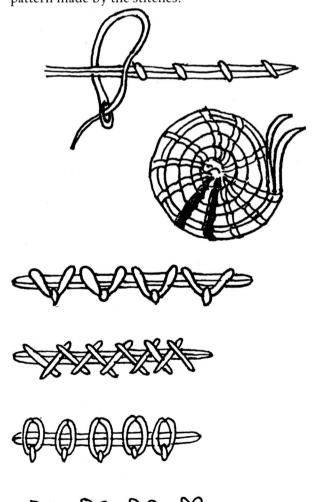

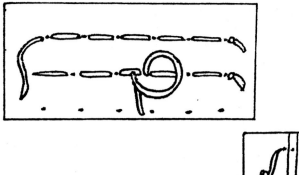

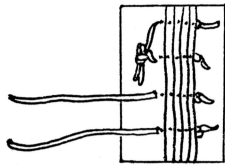

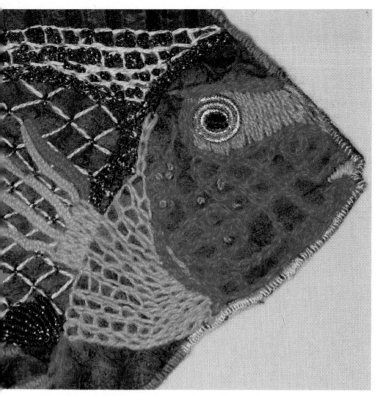

Gold and black thread couched with a cross stitch suggests scales and gold elastic thread couched in concentric circles creates the eye.

Tips for successful embroidery

Most embroidery looks good with two strands of six-strand embroidery thread. Bullion knots and french knots work well with two or three strands. If you require a bold effect, use many strands of embroidery thread or wool yarn. But use thread that is compatible with your ground fabric – silk on silk, cotton on cotton and so on.

Cut your thread about 20 cm (18 inches) long. If the thread is too long, it tends to tangle and knot. Begin and end with a few backstitches rather than with knots.

For a padded effect, work an outline of small running stitches around the shape and then fill in with two layers of satin-stitch. Keep your work clean and avoid pressing it as this will flatten the stitches.

A touch of smocking

Smocking is the embroidery used to hold together the tiny pleats on a gathered piece of fabric. It can be handy for a smocked dress on a little appliqué figure or even for a whole cushion cover.

Smocking is always worked before the article is put together. Generally the amount of fabric required is three times the width of the finished smocking. A printed transfer of smocking dots can be ironed onto the back of the fabric. Work a row of running stitches by hand across each row of dots and then pull up the threads to form folds ready for smocking. There are smock pleating machines available which automatically pick up and pleat the fabric.

Some useful smocking stitches
Rope stitch

This is a firm control stitch generally used on the border of the smocking. It is a stem stitch worked from the left with the thread above the needle picking up fabric on each fold. It can also be worked with the thread below the needle.

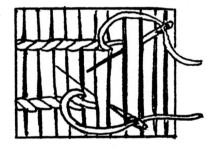

Cable stitch

This is a firm control stitch. Working from the left, pick up one fold with the thread above the needle and the next fold with the thread below the needle. Continue to the end of the row. This stitch can be repeated back to back to form a double cable.

Wave stitch

This is another firm control stitch. Work a zigzag pattern keeping the thread below the needle when working upwards and above the needle when working downwards. This stitch has many variations – it can be repeated in close rows or slightly open rows, in colour variations and in reverse to form a trellis.

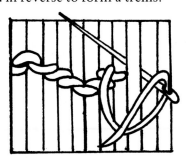

Chevron stitch

This is a stretch stitch. Backstitch the first and second folds together. Then slip the needle behind the second fold and pick up the fabric right to left on the line below. Backstitch the second and third folds together. Return the needle to the first line at the third fold and backstitch the third and fourth folds together. The thread must be above the needle on the first row and below the needle on the second row when making the backstitch. A diamond shape pattern can be achieved by working two rows of chevron.

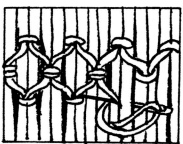

There are many more smocking combinations but these few stitches will come in handy if smocking is required in appliqué or patchwork.

Right A neat binding finish suits this type of quilt.

Below Bullion rosebuds and lazy daisy leaves look marvellous in a trellis or diamond pattern. Smocked cushions are something really special in an interior decorating scheme.

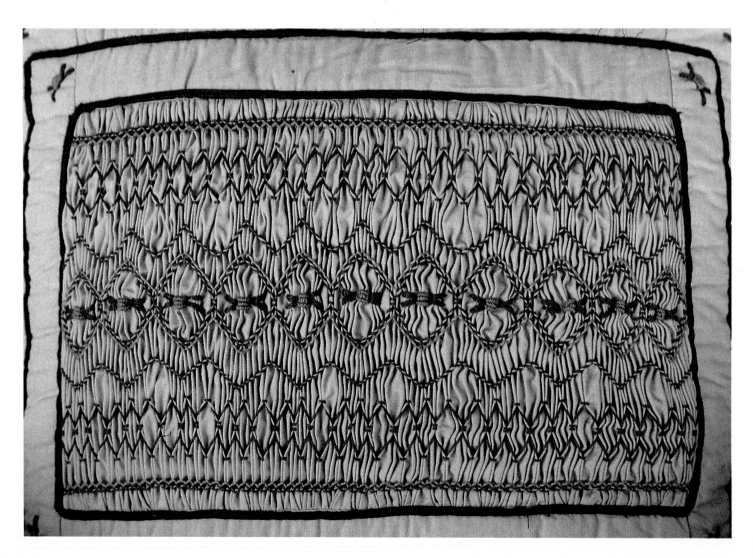

Binding quilts and pictures

A good way to finish quilts and pictures is to bind the edges with ready-made or self-fabric bias binding. To make self-fabric bias binding, cut strips of the background or quilt fabric on the bias. They should be at least 4 cm (1½ inch) wide. Lay the bias binding along the edge of the quilt or picture, right sides together, tack in position and stitch. Turn the binding over the edge, tuck under a small seam allowance and blind hem in place.

Another method of binding is to cut the lining top or ground fabric about 4 cm (1½ inch) larger all round than you want the finished quilt or picture to be. The excess can then be rolled over and blind hemmed in place. Mitre the corners for a professional finish.

Finishing with beads and sequins

Bead work can add a rich, exotic finish to a piece of appliqué or crazy patchwork. Beads and sequins catch the light and give extra dazzle to a design. There is a fantastic selection of beads available from rhinestones to flower-shaped sequins. The beading can be very subtle – for example, it can be used for the eye of an appliquéd fish. Or it can be done heavily – on a crazy patchwork bag or glamorous evening jersey, for example. Beads should be placed neatly together in pre-arranged order. They can be attached to the ground fabric or they can hang free in dense clusters.

I recommend three basic bead types – tiny glass seed beads in a variety of colours (transparent and opaque), bugle beads in various lengths and colours and sequins in all shapes and sizes.

Applying beads

Bead needles are long and thin with a tiny eye, and they are essential. Your thread choice will depend on the article and the desired effect. If the thread is to show, choose something decorative such as a contrasting colour or a metallic thread. Otherwise use a transparent nylon thread or a self-coloured thread. When using ordinary thread, a double strand is advisable.

Couching beads

Bring the needle through the fabric and thread on it a number of beads. Pull the thread through. Position the first bead on the ground fabric and with a separate needle and thread make a holding stitch close to the bead over the first thread. Slide the second bead up to the first and continue couching the thread between each bead.

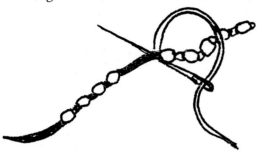

Seeding

Bring the needle through the fabric and thread three tiny beads onto it. Re-insert the needle into the fabric so that one bead rests on two. This technique is dynamic if a crusted area is worked.

Free-form/dangling beads

Secure the thread to the background and thread three bugle beads and one tiny bead on it. Then re-insert the needle through the bugle beads using the tiny bead as the anchor. Secure the thread to the background. Work any number of dangling clusters in this way.

Individual beads

Bring the needle through the fabric, thread the bead on to it and pull through. Insert the needle next to the first exit and make a stitch slightly longer than the bead with the thread below the needle. Pull through.

Many interesting combinations can be worked varying the beads and the lengths of the dangling sections.

Tiny beads can also anchor larger round beads if extra dimension is required.

Applying sequins
There are four ways of attaching sequins:

Single backstitch
Bring the needle through the fabric and thread the sequin. Hold the sequin in position and make a backstitch over the right side of the sequin. Bring the needle up again on the left of the sequin with enough space for the next sequin to fit edge to edge with the first sequin.

Far left This orchid shows seeding using large and small beads and sequins attached with a tiny bead.

Left This detail of the man's head shows a wonderful balance of large and small beads combining sequining and couching. A couple of dangling beads can be seen at the back of his head.

Top left The beaded bird's body was first appliquéd in blue suede and the beads were then worked to give a third dimension.

Above The beaded bird's tail is made with dangling beads. If used to embellish a jersey or T-shirt, the beads will move with the wearer.

Top right The leather appliqué shapes are decorated with dangling bugle and baby beads. The fall-away effect is achieved by increasing the number of bugles from one to five.

Double backstitch
Bring the thread through the fabric and the sequin. Make a backstitch over the right side of the sequin. Bring the needle out at the left side of the sequin and make a second backstitch through the eye of the sequin. Bring the needle out through the fabric leaving sufficient space for the next sequin. Continue sequining using two backstitches per sequin.

Invisible sequin stitch

Bring the needle through the fabric and sequin. Make a small stitch to the left over the sequin into the fabric. Come back up through the fabric leaving a small space half the size of the sequin. Thread on your second sequin and make a backstitch to meet the first sequin. Emerge again leaving a small space for the next sequin. The sequins must lap so that the rim covers the thread and the eye of the previous sequin.

Sequins and beads

Bring the needle through the fabric and the sequin. Thread on a tiny seed bead. Insert the needle back through the eye of the sequin and pull the thread tightly so that the tiny bead secures the sequin to the fabric. Experience, combining all your different bead types using linear designs, dangles and crusting.

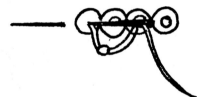

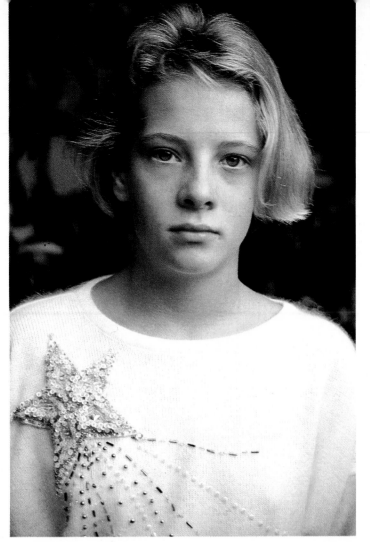

Far left above *An ordinary mohair jersey has been transformed into something quite unusual with a beaded star.*

Far left below *This is a stunning combination of appliqué, beading and embroidery.*

Left *Free rein has been given to colour and bead techniques in this design. Many different shapes and sizes of beads have been used. Some areas are worked with heavy crusting while other parts have a linear treatment. This is a combination of all bead techniques.*

Fabric painting and dyeing

One of the challenging aspects of appliqué and patchwork is to find the perfect piece of fabric. If the ideal piece is not available, a handy technique is to paint or dye your fabric.

Painting

There are many fabric paints available. The easiest to use is a ball-point tipped tube series which you can use on most fabric. In this series there is even a glue-based glitter paint which is ideal for extra dazzle on an appliquéd garment. Fabric paint must be used with restraint and not because it is easier or quicker than embroidering. A touch of paint for the blush on a cheek, a fine gold rim on a horizon or glitter on a star – these are paint details which count. Large areas can be painted using an aerosol spray can. Shapes can be masked and manipulated starting with light colours first.

Airbrushing and silkscreening are more expensive methods of applying paint to fabric.

Dyeing

Natural fabrics such as cotton, wool and silk dye well; man-made fibres do not take dye as successfully. There are cold dyes, multi-purpose dyes (suitable for use with hot water) and liquid dyes. The instructions for the different dyes are provided with them. Tea or coffee mixed with boiling water makes an excellent dye for changing white fabric to rich ecru.

Batik and tie-dyeing are techniques using dye to make designs on fabric. Batik is a very old method of dyeing fabric, which originated in Indonesia. It is a process in which patterns are drawn onto a piece of cloth with hot wax. The cloth is then dyed. The wax resists the dye and when it is removed, the design is revealed.

Tie-dyeing also works on the principle of resisting the dye in parts of the fabric. A piece of cloth is knotted, twisted or crumpled and then tied. When it is dipped into the dye, the colour penetrates only the untied area.

Special machine embroidery techniques

The more expensive sewing machines offer a host of embroidery techniques. Some of the most useful techniques for extra embellishments on appliqué and patchwork are discussed below.

Decorative discs or cams

The decorative discs can be repeated creating patterns such as rows of daisies, scalloped edges to create waves, feathery stitches for trees and fields. Many different patterns can be combined to give texture and interest to a dull piece of fabric. Some disc patterns are more solid than others and can be used to appliqué a raw edge to create a pattern and overlock simultaneously. Other discs produce a more linear pattern such as faggoting and feather stitching. Faggoting is a very attractive way of joining two pieces of material. It is ideal for machine patchwork. When doing faggoting, the two pieces of material must have seam allowances folded under so there are no raw edges. The shapes are put through the machine so that the thread catches both pieces of the fabric. Experiment using different types of thread.

Right above *This detail of a gymnast's head is a wonderful example of continuous rows of looping foot to give the effect of a silky head of hair.*

Far right above *The feet of the geese are made up of bullion knots and continuous chain stitch, and the chests are softened with looping foot.*

Right *An excellent example of creative stitchery using machine discs, twin needles and hand embroidery to enhance the appliqué.*

Left *Interesting effects are achieved using aerosol spray paint in combination with other techniques.*

Twin needle

This double needle fits onto all machines and is really a boon for decorative work. Many effects can be achieved. Working parallel lines of straight stitch with a twin needle gives the appearance of pin-tucking. Try it for wheat fields, a corrugated roof or a little pathway. Machine quilting using a twin needle gives a corded effect. Some machines have a serpentine setting which is exceptionally attractive when worked using a twin needle. With the twin needle, the designer can also play with different colour threads. The effect can be subtle if toning threads are used, or bold with bright complementary colours such as red and green on a white ground fabric.

Looping foot

This is a metal foot which has a shaft over which the thread is looped. The machine is set the same as for appliqué satin stitch – zigzag with a stitch width of about 2 and a stitch length from 0 to ½. Sew at a regular speed and guide the work according to the design required. When turning a sharp corner, lift the needle out of the fabric and raise the presser bar; gently push the loops off the shaft and swivel the fabric. Lower the presser bar and continue looping. The looping must be manually knotted off on completion.

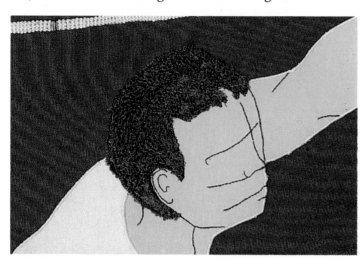

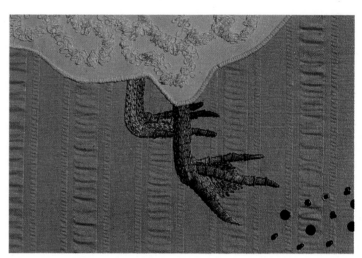

Woollen loops

Another method of making loops is to form a wire 'U' shape from a hanger. Wind your wool around the wire and machine straight stitch along the middle of the wool, sliding the wool loops off the hanger as you proceed. These loops can be machine stitched onto the appliqué.

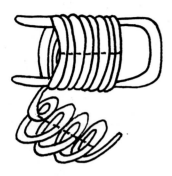

Couching on the machine

Braids, soutache or cord can be couched to the background using decorative machine stitches. Position the braid on the fabric and slowly machine over it, encasing the braid and securing it to the background.

Free-motion embroidery

Free-motion embroidery using straight stitch takes practice. The fabric can be stitched in an embroidery hoop but the hoop must be small enough to move under the needle without bumping the side of the machine. Place the fabric upside down in the hoop so that the fabric lies flat on the machine. Lower the feed dog, remove the presser foot and set the stitch length to zero. Lower the presser bar to engage the tension on the upper thread. Machine fairly fast and 'paint' with your needle, outlining and filling the design.

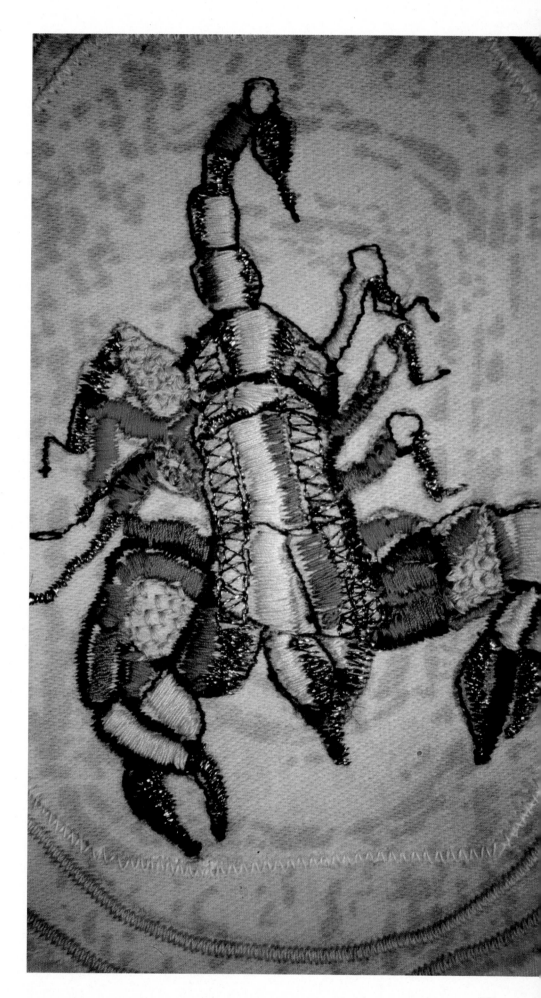

Above left *The chestnut horse from the appliqué below, highlighting the woollen loop mane.*

Left *Wool has been used to lift this design, and the result is a lovely, tactile quality. The wool has been looped, plaited and couched to give different effects.*

Right *This scorpion is entirely machine embroidered with satin stitch and disc work.*

Patchwork Basics

The colour harmony in this quilt has the effect of a Persian carpet. This quilt is a combination of moor's paving, flight of geese and saw tooth patchwork.

Patchwork is made by joining small patches of different fabrics together to form patterns. There are three very important factors in successful patchwork: a careful choice of fabric, the clever placement of patches and accurate joining.

The patches must be accurately cut and folded to achieve the geometric precision which is the essence of patchwork. The geometric design is the fine line between appliqué and patchwork. Although this chapter deals primarily with patchwork, do remember that patchwork, appliqué, quilting and embroidery are all part of the fabric fantasy. I will discuss the patchwork basics and provide some traditional designs and concepts, but I would like the reader to feel free to use this information and the templates provided to experiment and to incorporate patchwork with other fabric techniques.

Choosing the fabric

If you have a bag of scraps, sort through the pieces using the following tips as a guide:

- Choose fabrics that are washable and finely woven such as cottons so that they fold easily.
- Avoid loosely-woven fabrics which fray easily such as stretch fabrics and synthetics.
- Sort prints from plain fabrics. Small prints are more suitable than large ones.
- Fine wools, silks, fine linens and velvet are attractive but they are more difficult to handle.
- Leather is ideal because it does not fray. It is suitable for patchwork clothing but not for quilts.
- The fabric must be colour-fast.

This Ohio Star quilt is made up of a series of squares and triangles. There is an interesting balance of lights and darks in the design.

- The fabrics should be of similar types and all the same weight.
- If different fabrics are used together, the light-weight fabrics should be interfaced and the finished article should be dry-cleaned.
- Colours can be boldly contrasting or subtly shaded.
- Contrasts of dark and light give patch definition.
- Groups of pale patches can be assembled in blocks and bordered by dark patches or vice versa.
- One colour can be used throughout but with intensity to create the design.

If you do not have scraps, plan your design carefully and buy the exact colour scheme you require.

After choosing your colour scheme, decide on a pattern. If you are a beginner, choose a design with straight seams and few pieces to the block. Master the basics before tackling something too adventurous.

Templates

The next step is to buy or make a template for each pattern piece in the block. Home-made templates are cut from cardboard, hardboard or sandpaper, and they must be accurate if the patches are to meet properly. To make them you will need sharp pencils, scissors, graph paper and a set square, ruler, protractor and a pair of compasses. The template shape must be drawn on paper first and cut out. The paper pattern is then placed on the cardboard or other material being used for the template and very carefully cut around.

Templates can be made the exact size of the finished patch, in which case a 6 mm (¼ inch) seam allowance is added on the fabric. Or two templates are used – one template the size of the finished patch is used for the backing paper if required and another with the seam allowance included is used for the fabric. A window template is also handy. The window template is an empty frame; the outer edge is the size of the fabric patch with seam allowance included and the inner edge is the size of the backing paper.

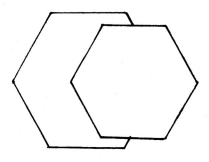

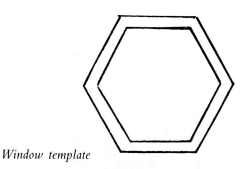

Set of templates for fabric and paper patches

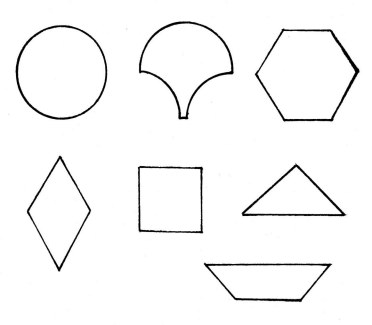

Window template

Most designs are based on a square. The square can be made into rectangles, more squares and triangles of different proportions, depending on how it is divided. Squares combined with triangles make more geometric shapes. Other designs are based on the circle or parts of the circle to produce polygons such as hexagons, pentagons or octagons. Because curved outlines are difficult to piece together, curved shapes are often appliquéd to square patches which are then pieced together. The following shapes are the most commonly used.

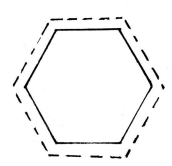

Single template – 6 mm (¼ in) must be added to the fabric

Preparing the patches

It is not absolutely necessary to use paper backings for the fabric patches, but paper does help to retain the shape of the fabric patches and makes the joining easier. Use paper that is neither too flimsy or thick: typing paper is an ideal weight or use pages from a glossy magazine. The purists prefer paper backing and hand patching, especially for hexagon and curved shapes. A very fine iron-on vilene interfacing can be used as a permanent backing. But do be careful that it is fine or the quilting might not produce the desired effect.

Paper backings are cut the exact size of the finished patch. Place the template on paper and draw around the shape with a pencil. Cut the paper as accurately as possible. For the fabric patches, place the template on the wrong side of the fabric and draw around the template. Be sure that the pattern is on the straight grain of the fabric, i.e. parallel to the selvage. Add a 6 mm (¼ inch) seam allowance of the fabric around each piece unless the template includes the seam allowance. Cut patches piece by piece for accuracy. Sort patches according to colour and shape. Each set of shapes or colour can be strung together on a length of thread or kept in a small box.

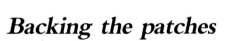

Stringing similar patches together

The many small curved pieces used in the double wedding ring design are clearly evident. The centre of each ring is superbly quilted with a floral motif that complements the basic design.

Backing the patches

The paper backing is attached to the fabric patch after both shapes have been cut out. Pin the paper patch to the centre of the wrong side of the fabric patch so that the edges of both patches are parallel. Fold the fabric edges over and tack the fabric to the exact size of the paper. Press the folds into position with an iron. When folding the edges of the triangles and diamonds, the points must be sharply formed. Circles and curved shapes are tacked around the fabric edge first. Then the paper patch is placed in the centre of the fabric and the tacking thread gently pulled until the circle gathers to fit the paper patch. Make a backstitch knot and cut the threads off.

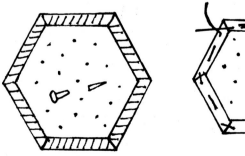

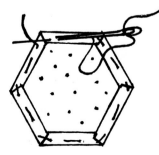

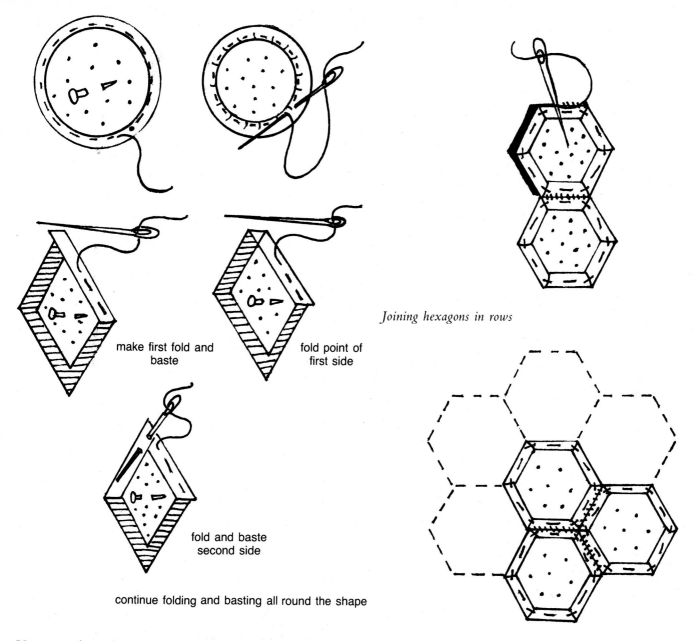

make first fold and
baste

fold point of
first side

fold and baste
second side

Joining hexagons in rows

continue folding and basting all round the shape

Your patchwork shapes are now ready to be pieced.

Joining hexagons in blocks

Piecing the patches

Piecing is the process of sewing all the small patchwork pieces together by hand or machine. The purists among quilters prefer hand piecing because it is traditional and very accurate. But some designs are very successful on the machine.

Piecing by hand

Complicated patchwork made up of many small pieces is best patched by hand. The paper backed fabric patches are joined together with small, evenly spaced overcasting stitches that are as invisible as possible. Patches are joined together in blocks in most quilts. But they can also be joined in rows or in one continuous piece. The type of patchwork and the shapes used will determine which method of joining is best.

Each block represents one complete pattern. Blocks are attached to each other in rows with tiny whip-stitches. Patterned blocks can also be alternated with solid-colour blocks, or joined with lattice bands to form a grid. When all the required rows are complete, join the rows by placing them right sides together and whip-stitching the edges together. Continue until the patchwork is complete. Iron the completed work and remove the tacking and paper patches.

If backing paper is not used, the patchwork pieces can be placed with right sides together and joined with a small, even running stitch. Begin and end with a back-stitch and maintain a perfect seam allowance of 6 mm (¼ inch). After sewing all the seams, press the seams to one side or open.

Machine piecing

Machine stitching is excellent for patchwork pieces with long, straight sides. It is less successful with curved patches and those with many short sides. Large squares and rectangles can easily be joined by machine. They do not require backing paper and can be placed with right sides together and machine straight stitched together. Join the patches side seam to side seam and then row to row. Maintain an exact 6 mm (¼ inch) seam allowance throughout and press the seams open and flat or to one side.

Complicated shapes such as the hexagon which have been backed with paper and tacked can be placed edge to edge right side up in the machine and joined with a zigzag stitch. Be sure that the needle catches both pieces of fabric.

Sewing corners and curves by hand or machine

Corners are unavoidable in some patchwork designs and practice is essential to do them correctly. Sew one seam right to the corner. Fasten off the thread and sew up to the corner from the other end. Either clip the corner and press the seam open and flat, or press the seams all one way if the fabric unravels easily.

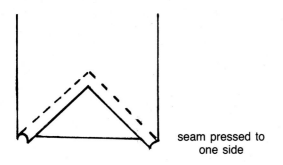

seam pressed to
one side

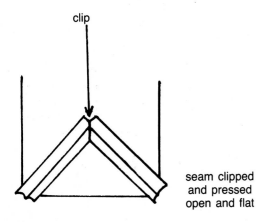

clip

seam clipped
and pressed
open and flat

If three pieces fit together in a corner, sew the first two pieces together up to the seam allowance. Sew the third piece up to the same point along each side and end off.

The corners can be trimmed if there is too much bulk.

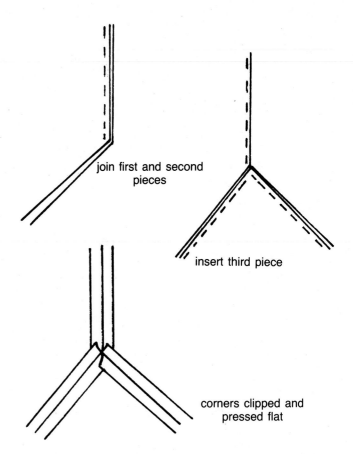

join first and second
pieces

insert third piece

corners clipped and
pressed flat

Curves in patchwork must be clipped and notched if they are to fit together properly. If the concave curves are notched and the convex curves are clipped, the seams can be turned under completely and the fabric will lie smoothly. Curves can be stay-stitched in the sewing machine to reinforce the shape before clipping and notching.

Finishing the patchwork

When all the blocks have been assembled, by hand or machine, the patched fabric must be finished off. You can construct fancy borders incorporating patterns from the main quilt, or the fabric can be lined and edged with a matching fabric bias binding. Lining alone is suitable only for small patchwork. Large patchwork should be quilted to stabilize the fabric and to add warmth.

Quilting your patchwork

Choose a quilting design that will enhance the patchwork and be compatible with the design. One popular form of quilting is outline quilting. The patchwork pieces are delineated by running stitches made 6 mm (¼ inch) on either side of the seam lines so each patch is outlined. These stitches secure the three layers together and give added dimension.

It is almost impossible to believe that heirlooms like these can be created from scraps.

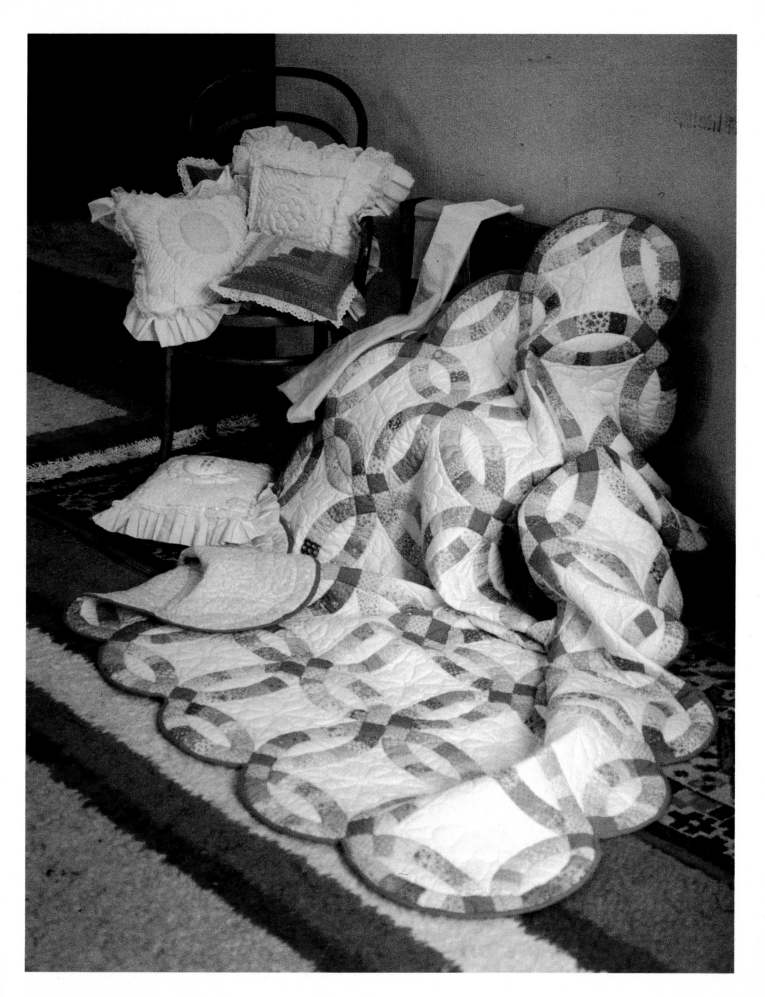

Diagonal quilting is also a popular pattern. Diagonal lines are stitched at regular intervals across the top of the quilt in one direction and then at the same intervals in the opposite direction forming a diamond pattern.

Quilting in patterns is the most decorative and elaborate form of quilting. Motifs can be made in many different shapes including flowers, hearts, shells, feathers and scallops. They can be used as single motifs or for repeated designs.

Transferring your quilt design

Use dressmaker's chalk, dressmaker's pencil, a special water soluble quilting pen or a soft lead pencil to trace your lines. If you use a pencil, press very lightly and make dotted rather than solid lines.

It is handy to make a template for intricate patterns such as shells, scallops or flowers. When the outlines of the templates have been marked, the details can be filled in. The motifs can be used individually or repeated to form border patterns.

This quilt is made of restful shades of green. Notice how the appliqué vintage cars are complemented by the quilt.

A few examples of quilting motifs

Some useful quilting diagrams

83

It is perfectly all right to combine several different quilting concepts. The pieced blocks can be quilted along the seam lines, plain blocks can be quilted in patterns, and the border can be stitched in diamonds.

Many interesting combinations can be used as long as the quilting complements the patchwork.

Before quilting, three layers are sandwiched together – first the lining, wrong side up, then the wadding and finally the patchwork top, right side up. Tack your quilt together from the centre and radiate out towards the corners. (See p50 for illustration.) The quilt is now ready to be quilted by hand or machine.

Hand quilting

Hand quilting can be done on a quilting hoop or on a floor frame. The quilting hoop is like a large embroidery hoop with an inner hoop that is placed under the quilt and an outer hoop that fits on top. It has screws which can be adjusted to accommodate any thickness and can be tightened to hold the quilt taut. Begin quilting from the centre of the quilt and work outwards to the edges.

A floor frame is essential if a group of people are going to work on a quilt or if the quilt is very large. A floor frame comprises two long poles and side braces and is supported on a stand or trestles. The quilt is stretched between the poles and braces.

For hand quilting, use a waxed quilting thread and a sharp needle. Cut the thread about 46 cm (18 inches) long and use it single. The thread should match the ground fabric. The running stitches must be short and even. A leather thimble is helpful when pushing the needle through three layers of fabric.

Machine quilting

Machine quilting may be faster than hand quilting but often the size of the quilt makes machine quilting extremely uncomfortable. It is often better to machine quilt individual blocks and let the quilt grow as each quilted block is attached to the next. The three layers (lining, wadding and patchwork top) must be well tacked. Drop the feed dog when placing the quilt in the machine. Raise the feed dog and set the machine on a fairly long straight stitch (about 3½ on most machines). Using standard mercerized sewing thread, machine quilt, row by row, from the centre outward. Gently guide the quilt – if you pull, it will pucker badly. A quilting foot can be handy because it has a built-in space bar that makes straight line stitching easier.

Tied and buttoned quilting

Tied quilting is another method of sewing the patchwork, wadding and lining together. The three layers are knotted together at regular intervals. It is quicker than stitched quilting but not as decorative. Tightly knotted bows or buttons can be used instead of knots. Use an embroidery needle and wool or embroidery thread. Make one stitch through all the layers, leaving a long end on top of the quilt. Make a backstitch and bring the needle up to the top again. Tie the ends together making a strong knot or tie them together in a tight bow.

Tied quilting

Buttons can also be used. Secure a button on the top side. Pass the needle through all the layers and connect another button on the underside. Come back through all the layers and pull the thread firmly through both buttons and all the layers of the fabric. Secure the thread pulling the buttons down to give a 'puffy' effect.

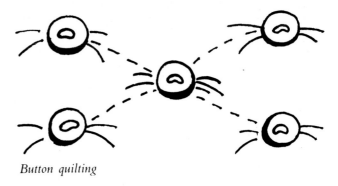

Button quilting

For more quilting ideas such as cording and trapunto, see p50-52.

Finishing off

There are many different ways of finishing off a quilt. The simplest is to fold the top fabric over the wadding, and the bottom layer under the wadding so that the two edges meet neatly and then to whip-stitch or top-stitch them together.

A commercial bias binding or fabric binding gives a lovely finish and is particularly suitable for curved edges. Pin the bias binding to the quilt top, right sides together, and sew all round the quilt. Then fold the binding to the back, pin in place and blind hem.

French binding is stronger than single fabric binding. Cut bias strips four times the width of the finished border with an extra 6 mm (¼ inch) for a seam allowance. Fold the strips in half lengthwise with the wrong sides together. Iron the strip, position it on the quilt top and attach it using the same method as for commercial bias binding.

French binding

The backing fabric or lining can also be used to border raw edges. Cut the fabric larger than the quilt top. You will require double the width of the finished border plus 12 mm (½ inch) for seam allowance. The wadding must also be larger than the quilt top. Extend it beyond the quilt top to the width of the finished border. Fold the backing over the wadding and lap it onto the quilt top with the raw edge turned under. Tack the band in position, mitring the corners. Machine top stitch or hand hem this edge. Slip-stitch the mitred corners. Reverse this procedure to make a binding from the quilt top.

A frill is a very pretty way of finishing a quilt. It can be double or hemmed depending on the desired effect. Measure the border lengths of the quilt and cut the frill twice this length. Using a gathering stitch on the machine, sew two lines of stitches just inside the edge.

Pull up the gathering threads and fit the ruffle to the quilt top, right sides together. Machine stitch in place. Position your lining over the quilt top and ruffle and machine stitch round leaving a small opening for turning through. Slip-stitch the opening closed.

The gathered frill adds to the olde worlde charm of the quilt.

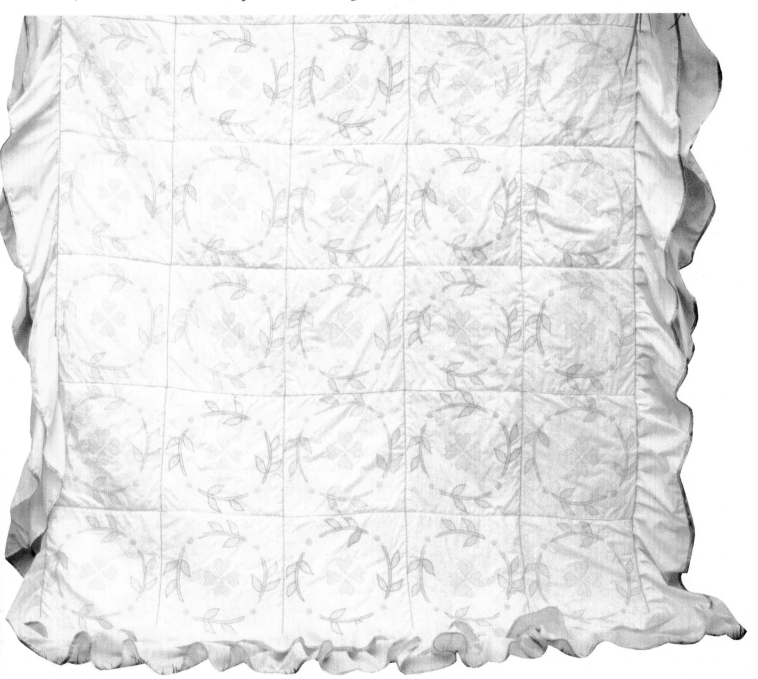

A Selection of Popular Patchwork Designs

This design's colour vibrations will change according to the choice of fabric. Accuracy in cutting is fundamental for a design like this to succeed. This is patchwork with a difference. It has not been traditionally patched but appliquéd. It is a 3-D block patchwork design.

Hand patchwork

This chapter provides patterns suitable for hand patching. A beginner should choose a design with straight seams and few pieces to the block. Make a cushion before a quilt. When you have learned all the skills, you can tackle complicated combinations with curves and many pieces. Or you may want to combine patchwork, appliqué and quilting to create an heirloom.

The templates provided are a mixture of squares, diamonds, triangles and circles. If you choose a combination of different templates on one quilt be sure that the sizes work together and fit into your overall pattern. For example, if 'drunkard's path' is the centre and 'flying geese' the border, you might have to alter the size of the border templates to suit your measurements.

There are a few patchwork designs, such as cathedral window, yo-yo, shell and log cabin, that are pieced together in different ways from standard patchwork. Cathedral window, yo-yo and shell are hand patched and the procedure for piecing them is described below. Log cabin is very successfully joined in the machine. See p103 for the procedure to use.

Cathedral window

Cathedral window patchwork is a patched and quilted surface achieved by folding squares of plain cotton as frames over smaller squares of contrast or printed fabric.

This patchwork gives an illusion of diamond-shaped windows.

Cut 23 cm (9 inch) squares of plain fabric and turn under a 6 mm (¼ inch) seam allowance on all sides. Hem.

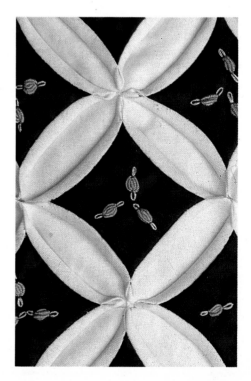

Left Cathedral window is essentially a hand-patched technique. Fascinating results are achieved by exploring the internal window shapes.

Below Embroidered bullion rosebuds create a focal point in the cathedral window.

With wrong side up, fold all four corners to the centre. Iron the folds and stitch the corners to the centre of the patch.

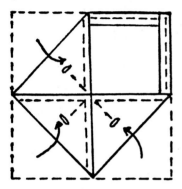

Fold all four corners of the new square to the centre again. Iron the folds.

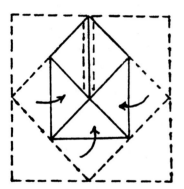

Fold all four corners of the new square to the centre again. Iron the folds.

Stitch the corners together through the centre making a neat cross stitch.

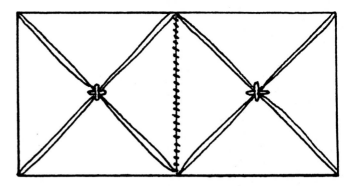

Make the required number of squares and whip-stitch the squares together in rows.

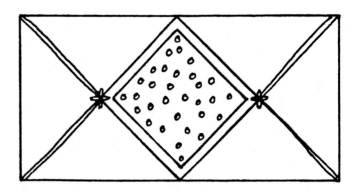

Cut 6 cm (2¼ inch) squares of contrast or printed fabric on the straight grain. Pin each square diagonally on top of the seam of two folded squares.

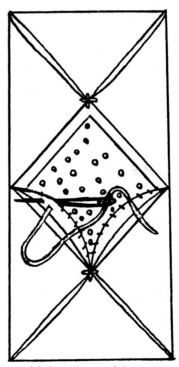

Fold the edges of the original squares over the diamond patches. Hem-stitch the edge through all the layers. Simply hem the outer edges or turn the edges in and hem half squares in position.

The first two steps can also be done in the sewing machine.

Fold your 23 cm (9 inch) square in half and machine straight stitch each end with a 6 mm (¼ inch) seam allowance

Fold each of the unstitched edges in half so that all four corners meet in the centre. Machine stitch the unstitched edges up to the middle but leave a small space free for turning through. Trim the seams, clip the corners, turn through and press into a square shape. Continue with steps 3 to 8.

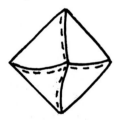

The centre of the squares can be embroidered for extra embellishment. The folded squares when finished are 10 × 10 cm (4 × 4 inches). Sixteen squares joined in four rows of four makes a perfect cushion.

Yo-yo

Using the template, cut out a circle of fabric with a 7.5 cm (3 inch) diameter. Turn under 6mm (¼ inch) and with a double thread make small running stitches all round the edge. Pull the turned-under edge of the circle into tight gathers and secure by tying the two ends of the thread. Press the circles and arrange your pattern. Join the circles with a few overcast stitches.

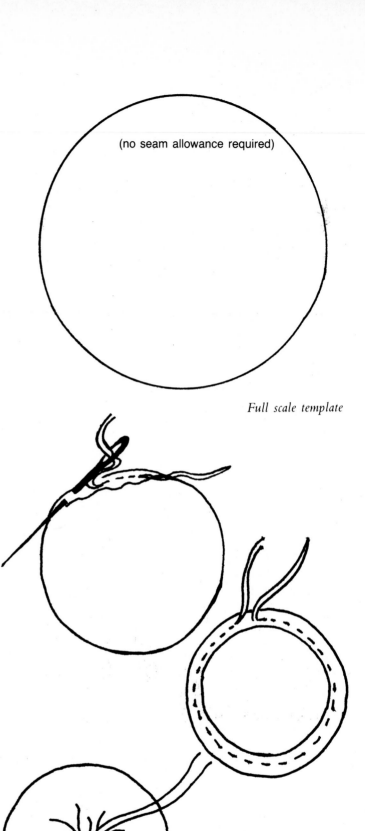

(no seam allowance required)

Full scale template

Shell pattern

Make a fabric shape using the template and adding 6 mm (¼ inch) seam allowance all round. Cut out iron-on vilene patches from the template (no seam allowance required) and iron them onto the wrong side of the fabric. Fold over the curved edge and tack in place. Plan your colour sequence; the shell shapes are joined in rows. Place a row of basted patches along the top of a back-ground fabric. Position the second row so that it overlaps the first and covers the stems. Tack and then hem-stitch around the curves of the second row of shells, catching the fabric of the first row. Continue row by row until the patchwork is the required length. Use half patches at the edges. On the final row cut the stems off, fold the edges under and hem.

Iron-on vilene

This template will make a 40 cm (16 in) block if pieced as in the accompanying diagram.

Hexagons

Many different effects can be achieved using the hexagon shape depending on the materials used and the arrangement of colours. The hexagons can be joined in rows or in rosettes. Add 6 mm (¼ inch) seam allowance on all patterns.

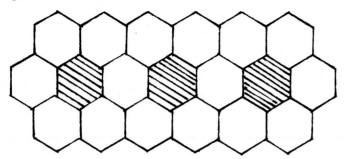

Rosette border

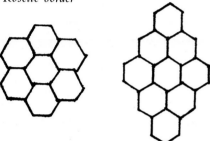

Rosette   *Diamond*

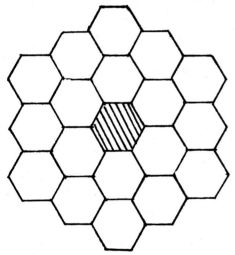

Grandmother's flower garden

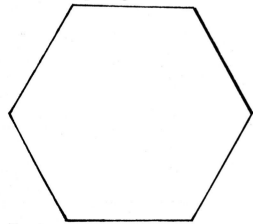

Template

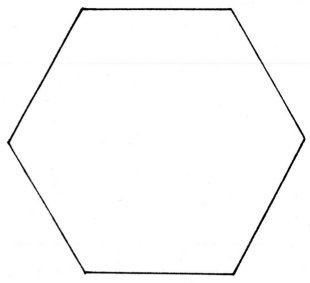

Template

Diamonds, squares and triangles

Add 6 mm (¼ inch) seam allowance.

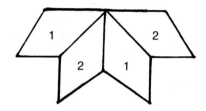

Diamond star

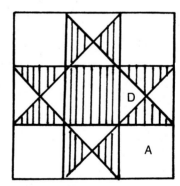

Ohio star

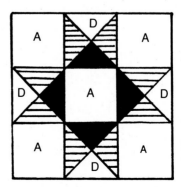

Variable star

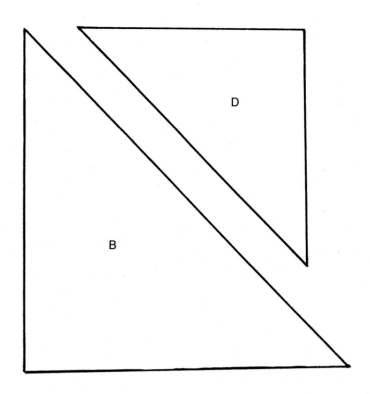

D

B

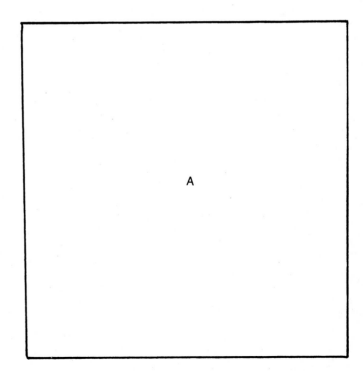

A

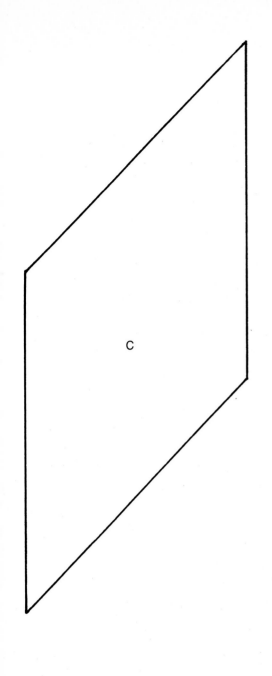

C

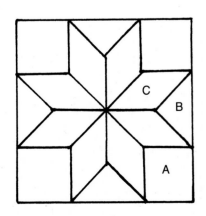

C

B

A

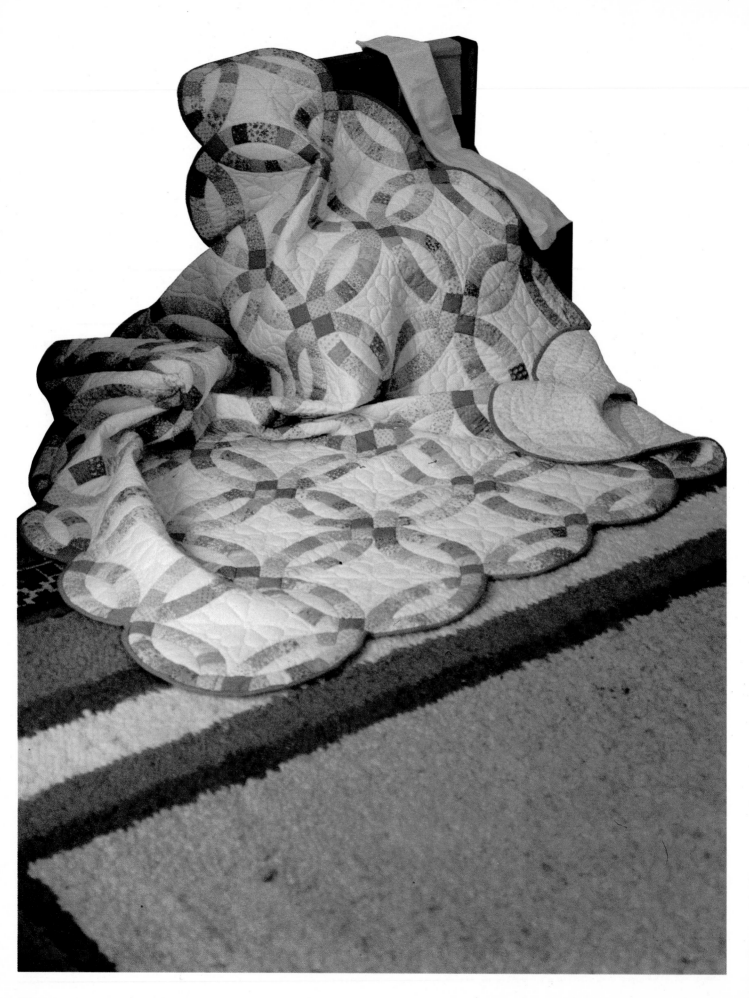

Double wedding ring

This is a fairly difficult patchwork. Join all Bs, Cs and Ds. Then sew them to A. Finally join to E. This design gives a beautiful scalloped edge with half round corners. The diameter of the wedding ring block is 3.5 cm (1.4 inches). The central medallion lends itself to pattern quilting. Add 6 mm (¼ inch) seam allowance on all pieces.

The intersecting rings on a double wedding ring quilt create a superb scalloped border. This is an advanced patchwork because of the curved shapes and the vast number of small patches.

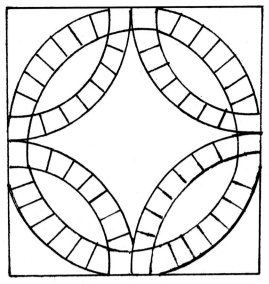

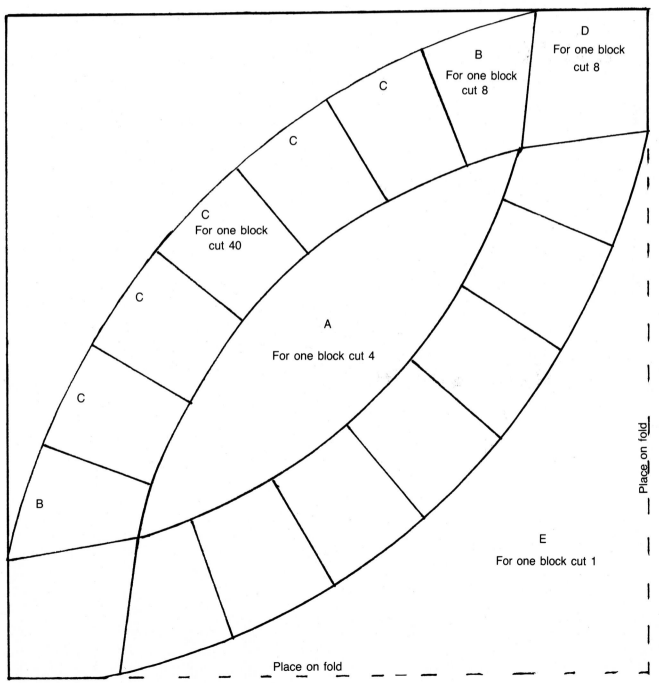

D
For one block
cut 8

B
For one block
cut 8

C

C

C
For one block
cut 40

C

C

B

A

For one block cut 4

E
For one block cut 1

Place on fold

Place on fold

Drunkard's path

Cut out eight large patches and eight small patches in a dark fabric. Do the same with a light fabric. Piece two shapes in contrasting colours edge to edge to form a small square. Then piece all the squares together to form the 30 cm (12 inch) block using the piecing diagram as a guide. If two different darks are used, you can run all of one colour in a diagonal line in one direction and all of the other colour in a diagonal line in the opposite direction.

Moor's paving is a variation.

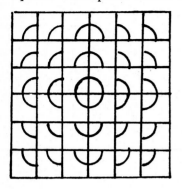

Moor's paving

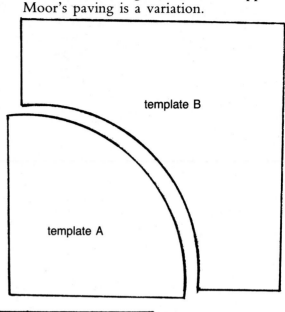

template B

template A

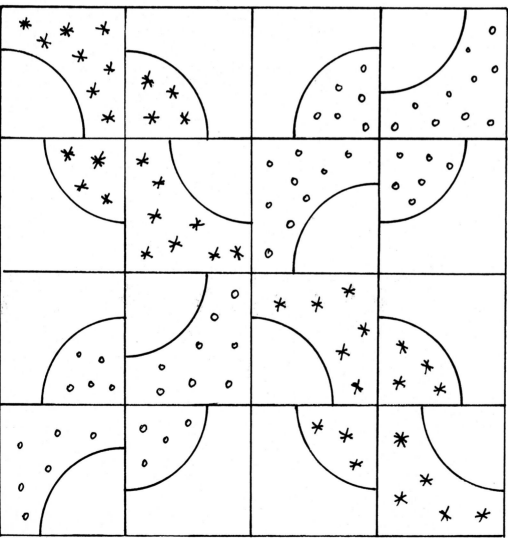

Drunkard's path

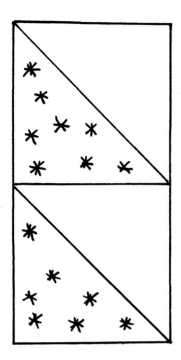

Sawtooth border

Super border designs

These two triangles make several excellent border designs. The large triangle placed back to back creates the sawtooth design. The small triangle combined with the large one forms the flying geese. Add 6 mm (¼ inch) seam allowance all round. The finished geese will be about 12 cm (4¾ inches) wide.

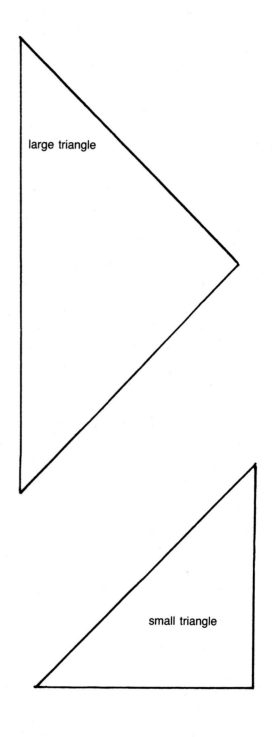

large triangle

small triangle

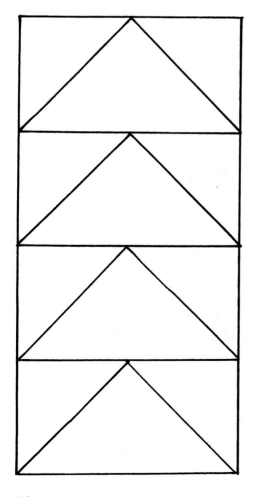

Flying geese

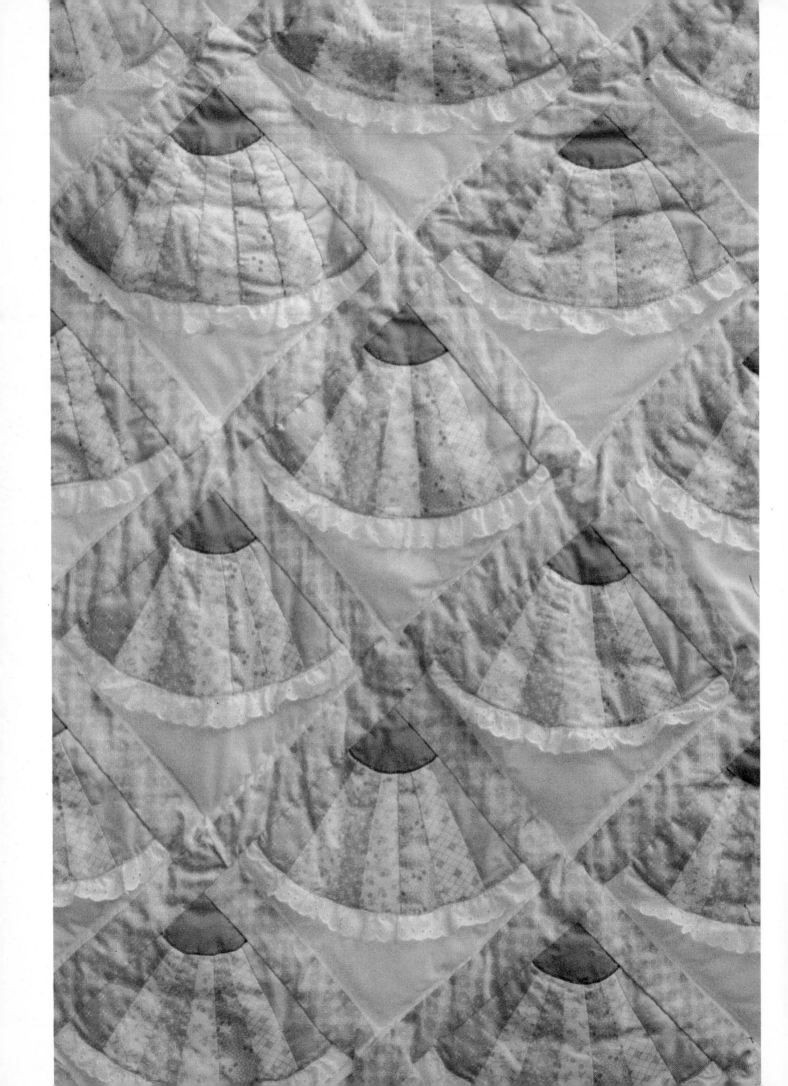

Machine patchwork

Machine patching is quicker and stronger than hand patching but not quite so traditional. Most of the hand patchwork designs can be pieced by machine, but straight edged designs are more suitable than those with curved edges.

Some designs, such as Dresden plate and grandmother's fan, can be machine pieced and then appliquéd to the ground fabric. See pp107 and 108 for templates and instructions for these designs.

Left *This is a diagonal variation of the grandmother's fan design. It is very successful hand or machine patched.*

Hand patched details of the grandmother's fan design.

Each piece of the Dresden plate design can be machine patched and then appliquéd to the background.

Bear's paw

Bear's paw is a straight-edged patchwork combining squares, triangles and rectangles. The pieced patchwork makes a 35.5 cm (14 inch) block. Using the templates and sketch provided, cut the following pieces for each block. The templates include the seam allowance.

In background colours:

- 4 of A
- 16 of C
- 4 of D

In main colour:

- 1 of A
- 4 of B
- 16 of C

For one block, join 16 pairs of C to make squares (sixteen squares).

Join the two squares together to make four sets of and four sets of . Join four sets of to one A square to make four sets of . Join four B squares to to make Join four sets of to make four complete paws.

Now assemble the four paws and the central strips to form one block.

Join 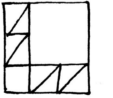 to [A] to [grid]

Join [A] to [A] to [A]

Join [grid] to [A] to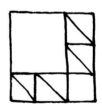

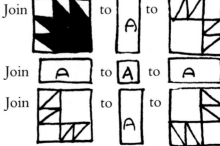

This block makes a lovely cushion. To make a quilt continue making a number of blocks and join the blocks in rows until the quilt is the required size. Flying geese makes a good border for bear's paw.

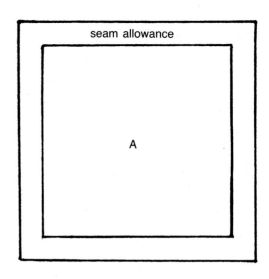

seam allowance

A

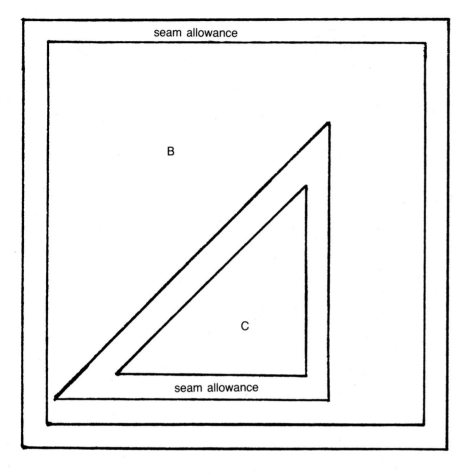

seam allowance

B

C

seam allowance

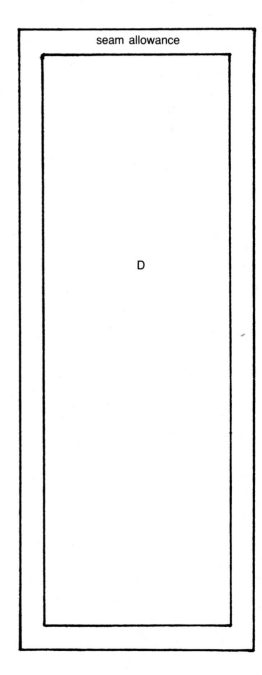

seam allowance

D

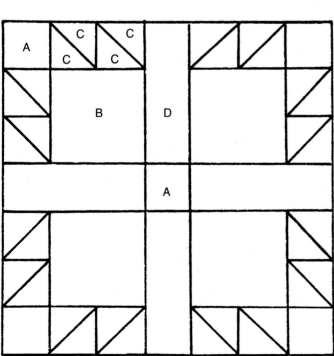

A

C C

C C

B

D

A

Left Bear's paw
patchwork is a
combination of squares,
triangles and rectangles.

Log cabin (see page 105 for templates)

Log cabin is extremely decorative and can be machine patched most successfully. It is worked in square blocks composed of half light and half dark strips stitched and folded around a small centre square. The focal point is the central square and it must contrast with the light and dark strips. To make a block of log cabin patchwork, you must start with a foundation fabric. Cut a calico square the size of the finished block, 25 × 25 cm (10 × 10 inches), plus 6 mm (¼ inch) seam allowance all round. Fold and press two diagonal lines from corner to corner on the square to help position the strips. Then cut out and apply the strips as follows:

Cut the small centre square with 6 mm (¼ inch) seam allowance. Pin the small square to the centre of the large square.

Using templates 1 and 2 and adding 6 mm (¼ inch) seam allowances all round, cut pieces in light fabric. Place strip 1, face down, over the central square. Machine straight stitch through all layers 6 mm (¼ inch) from the edge.
Fold back the first strip and press lightly. Secure strip 2 in the same way as the first.
Using templates 3 and 4 and adding 6 mm (¼ inch) seam allowance, cut pieces in dark fabric. Secure and fold these dark strips in the same way. This completes the first circuit.
Prepare and secure the remaining strips in the same way, maintaining the light and dark colour patterning throughout.

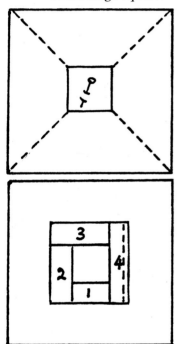

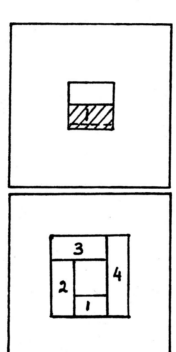

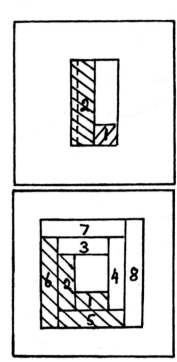

When the required number of blocks have been made, join them in rows by placing the right sides together and stitching with a 6 mm (¼ inch) seam allowance.

The positioning of the dark and light halves of the blocks forms different variations of the log cabin pattern: medallions, open diamonds (barn raising), zigzag, diagonals and windmills.

Variations can also be achieved by attaching the strips in different ways. In the courthouse steps patterns, the light and dark strips are opposite each other instead of adjacent. And in the pineapple pattern, they are worked round a central square with straight and diagonal lines. To make the pineapple pattern, proceed in the same way as for the standard log cabin, but at the end of each circuit place four strips diagonally at each corner.

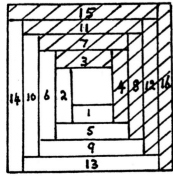

Standard log cabin

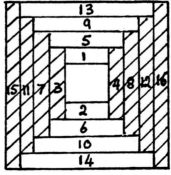

Courthouse steps

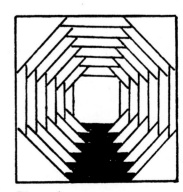

Pineapple

103

Log cabin patchwork can be machine quilted by stitching on the seams of each strip forming radiating squares.

Top *Placing strips in the staircase variation of log cabin patchwork.*

Above *Another log cabin variation: at the end of each circuit place four strips diagonally at each corner to give the spiky effect of the pinapple.*

Left *This is a barn raising variation of log cabin patchwork.*

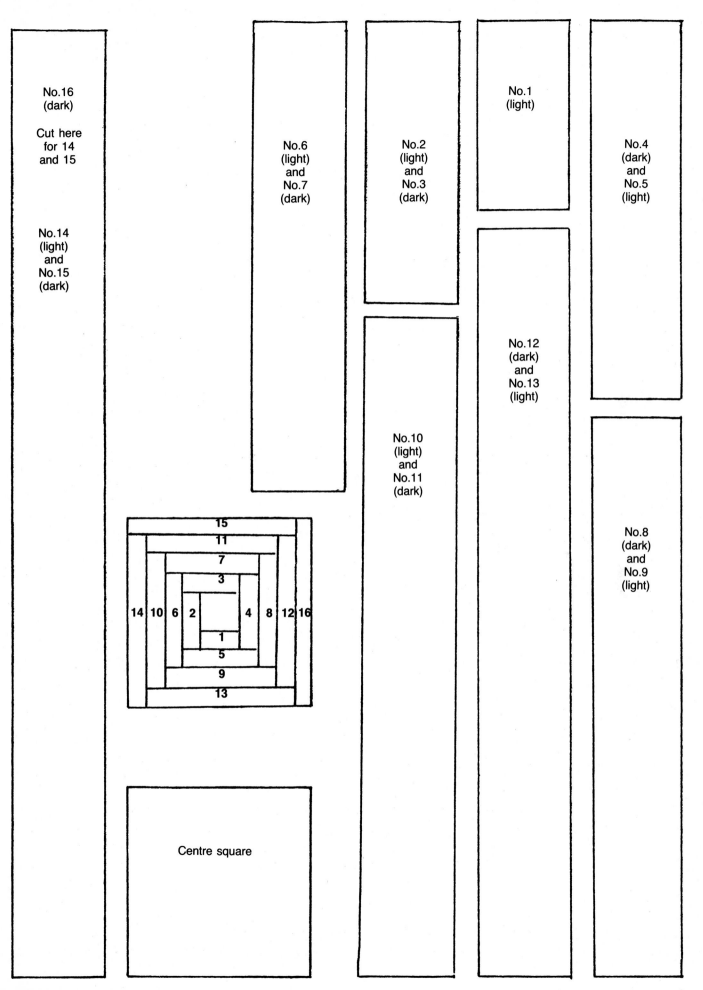

No.16
(dark)

Cut here
for 14
and 15

No.14
(light)
and
No.15
(dark)

No.6
(light)
and
No.7
(dark)

No.2
(light)
and
No.3
(dark)

No.1
(light)

No.4
(dark)
and
No.5
(light)

No.12
(dark)
and
No.13
(light)

No.10
(light)
and
No.11
(dark)

No.8
(dark)
and
No.9
(light)

15
11
7
3
14 10 6 2 4 8 12 16
1
5
9
13

Centre square

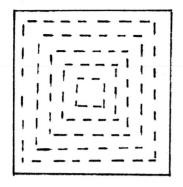

Machine stitch all round the square. Continue making more squares like this until there are enough for one row. Position the squares, right sides together, and machine stitch. Having made one row, slash the back of one square and gently stuff some polyester wadding into the cavity until a well-rounded puff forms on the fabric side.

stuff wadding into cavity from the back

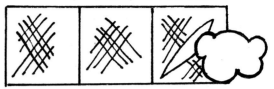

Close the muslin back with tiny whipping stitches. Continue slashing and stuffing each square. Make more rows in the same way and then join row by row until the quilt is the required size. The quilt can be finished off with a frilled edge and then lined.

Stuffed patchwork (Puff Quilt)
To make a cosy cot quilt cut a piece of muslin 8.5 cm (3½ inches) square. Now cut a piece of fabric 11.5 cm (4½ inches) square. Place the fabric square over the muslin, pinning at the corners. Make small pleats at the centre of each of the four sides so that the fabric fits the muslin exactly.

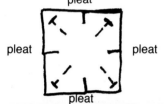

This puff quilt is really cosy and many different designs can be created by planning your fabrics and arranging them in a pattern.

Dresden plate

This design is excellent for machine patching. Join the panels and then appliqué the circle in position. Appliqué the patchwork onto a 38 cm (15 inch) block. The panels make an attractive scalloped border.

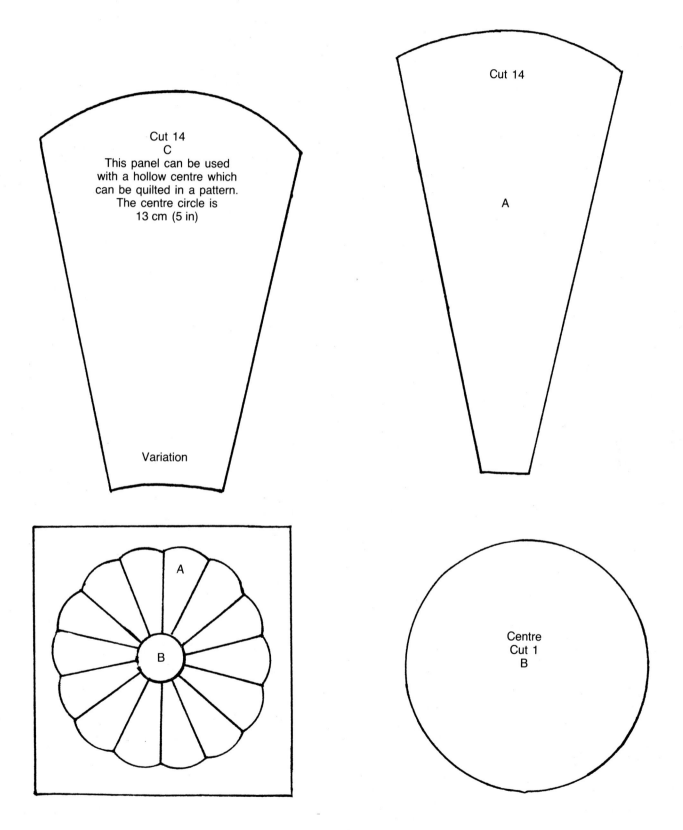

Cut 14

Cut 14
C
This panel can be used with a hollow centre which can be quilted in a pattern. The centre circle is 13 cm (5 in)

A

Variation

A

B

Centre
Cut 1
B

Grandmother's fan

This patchwork can be pieced by hand or machine and then appliquéd onto a plain block. Great fun can be had by adding lace frills to make it look really old fashioned. Add 6mm (¼ inch) seam allowance.

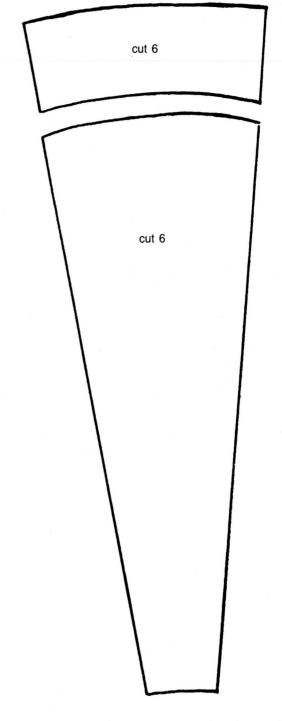

cut 6

cut 6

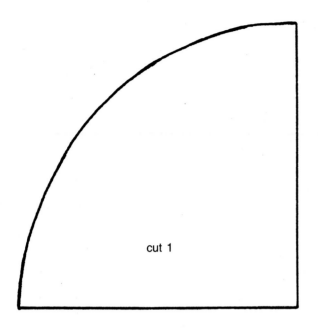

cut 1

Block variations

When cutting out patches based on templates for block variations, add 6 mm (¼ inch) seam allowance.

3D block patchwork can be pieced in the traditional way with seam allowances. A completely untraditional method is to prepare and assemble the squares and diamonds as for appliqué and then to attach them by satin stitching along the raw edges.

A Vasarely variation

The templates and piecing diagrams in this book should be stepping stones to designing your own quilt. The photographs and illustrations should act as inspiration. In designing, keep in mind that the finished blocks usually cover only the top of the mattress. A border is added for the overhang; its width depends on how much overhang you require on each side. The following mattress measurements will assist you when planning a quilt:

    Cot 70 × 127 cm (27 × 50 in)
    Single bed 91 × 190 cm (36 × 75 in)
    Double bed 137 × 190 cm (54 × 75 in)
    Queen size 150 × 203 cm (60 × 80 in)
    King size 183 × 203 cm (72 × 84 in)

Patchwork can be machine pieced and hand quilted, or machine pieced and machine quilted, hand pieced and hand quilted or machine pieced, appliquéd and quilted.

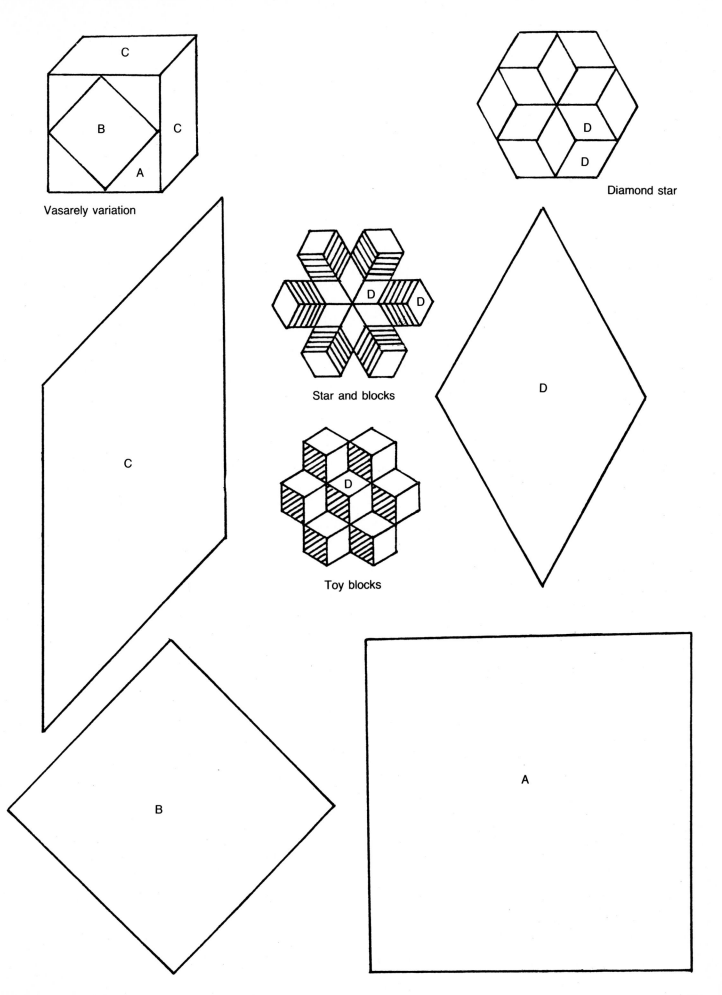

Vasarely variation

Diamond star

Star and blocks

Toy blocks

Projects

This quilt is one of the largest and most ambitious of the
practical and decorative projects which follow.

Materials for appliqué, patchwork and quilting

Supplies and equipment

Pencils
soft lead pencil (B or HB)
dressmaker's pencil (pink, white or blue)

Threads
Mercerized threads for machining and tacking
A selection of embroidery thread
Quilting thread

Needles
An assorted packet of sewing needles including crewel for fine work, chenille for medium work, a curved upholstery needle and long, fine beading needles

Machine needles
A selection including a fine, sharp needle for general appliqué, a leather needle, a ball-point needle for stretch fabrics, a denim needle for very thick fabric, a twin-needle and a looping needle. All these needles are available for all sewing machines

Beeswax
Beeswax to coat the thread so that it will pull easily through closely woven fabrics and leather. It also strengthens the thread and holds the strands together (especially metallic thread)

Scissors
1 pair of small, fine-pointed scissors
1 large pair of dressmaker's scissors

Pins
Sharp and fine dressmaker's (straight) pins
Coarse pins to mark the fabric
Safety pins in various sizes for threading lace, ribbon or cord

Embroidery and quilting rings (hoops)

Transfer materials

Iron-on vilene (nonwoven interfacing)
Cardboard or X-ray plate for templates
Drawing paper and tracing paper

Fabric and trimmings

Once you have begun to create, your collection of fabrics and trimmings will grow. Become a magpie. Gather and hoard all the bits and pieces you can. Never say 'no' to an offer of remnants from a fellow dressmaker. Start to see fabric in terms of texture, design and images. Buy small pieces of beautiful fabric and trimming when you see them and eventually, when you create, you will have just about everything you need in your own fabric treasure chest.

Appliqué and patchwork fabrics

cotton in various colours and patterns (pre-shrunk, colour fast)
wools
linen
leather
sheers (nylon, organza)
silks
satin
net
high pile fabrics such as velvet, corduroy
chintz
remnants of fancy fabrics – sequined, beaded, ribboned
wadding and muslin for quilting

Trimming

lace – old and new (cotton, broderie-anglaise, nylon)
braid (ric-rac, bias binding, piping, soutache, cord etc.)
ribbon
buttons
beads and sequins

The following projects are in order of increasing complexity. Many of the projects use the double vilene technique described on p36 and recommend particular embroidery stitches, which are given on pp58-64.
Most of the designs need to be enlarged: for methods see page 19.

A good clear working area, assembled equipment and you're ready to begin.

113

Appliqué pockets or yokes

Any small design looks charming on children's clothing, especially on pockets or yokes. These designs are excellent for beginners.

Materials for 2 pockets

Fabric
scraps of pre-shrunk cotton in different colours
4 22 cm (9 in) squares of dungaree fabric for the pockets
30 cm (10 in) iron-on vilene interfacing

Thread
matching machine thread

Trimmings
a small packet of tiny black beads

Instructions
Trace the design. Prepare for machine appliqué and assemble onto one layer of pocket fabric. Machine satin-stitch in matching colours. Bead the centre of the daisies with tiny black beads. With right sides together, stitch the back of each pocket onto the appliquéd fronts, leaving a small opening to turn through. Trim seams, clip corners, turn through and top-stitch.

Materials for yoke (cup ckae)

Fabric
small pieces of pre-shrunk cotton in white, shocking pink, lilac and red

Thread
matching machine thread

Trimmings
a selection of rhinestones

Instructions
Trace the design and prepare and assemble the pieces onto the yoke. Machine satin-stitch the pieces in place. Attach the rhinestones to the cake.

115

A happy clown

This is another quick and easy appliqué project. Imagine this happy fellow in a nursery on a cot duvet, continental pillow-slip or as a wall hanging. He would even cheer up a drab nursery-school playroom.

Materials

Fabric

1 m (40 in) navy blue chintz for the background
30 cm (10 in) white chintz for the face and hands
30 cm (10 in) red cotton for the hat, nose and pantaloon inserts
50 cm (20 in) patterned cotton for the shirt
50 cm (20 in) striped cotton for the pantaloons
small scraps of pink cotton for the cheeks, blue cotton for the braces, yellow cotton for the socks and green cotton for the shoes
1 m (1 yd) iron-on vilene interfacing

Thread

red, blue, yellow, white and green machine thread
black, white, blue and red embroidery cotton

Trimmings

2 "arty" buttons
1 m (40 in) each of green, blue, yellow and red 2.5 cm (1 in) wide satin ribbon for the ruffle
1 m (40 in) narrow spotted ribbon for the shoe laces
1 ball yellow wool for the pom-pom

Instructions

Enlarge the design overleaf. Prepare vilene-backed shapes and tack them directly onto the background. Machine satin-stitch using matching thread colours. Use the looping foot on the machine for the hair. Set your machine on a long, straight stitch for gathering. Make two rows of gathering stitches in each of the ribbons for the ruffle. Draw up these threads until the ribbons fit comfortably below the clown's face. Hand sew the ruffles in place. Embroider the eyes in continuous chain-stitch and the eyebrow line and ears with a small back-stitch. The mouth is red satin-stitch. Attach bows and buttons. Make the yellow pom-pom.

To make a pom-pom, draw two circles, one inside the other, on a double layer of cardboard (see diagram). Cut out the inner circle and wind the wool around the double ring of cardboard until the centre cannot hold any more wool. With sharp scissors cut the wool along the outer edge of the double ring. Pull the rings apart slightly and tie another piece of wool tightly around the centre, between the rings. Remove the cardboard and fluff out the pom-pom.

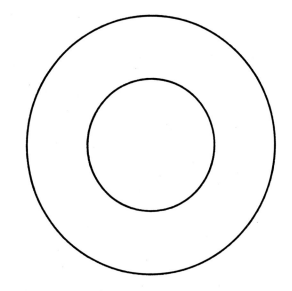

Running shoes

This quick and easy design for running shoes is suitable for any sport-loving family. It would look great in a teenage bedroom and, if dad jogs, even in the study. The padded soles and real shoe laces give a super third dimension. This design could be used as a picture, on a sports bag, in the centre of a quilt or on a cushion.

Materials

Fabric
50 cm (20 in) cream cotton for the background
30 cm (10 in) dark blue cotton for the running shoes
a small piece of white, ready-quilted cotton for the shoe soles
If ready-quilted fabric is not available, a small piece of wadding and white fabric will do for the padded sole
small scraps of suede in beige, yellow and blue
50 cm (20 in) of iron-on vilene interfacing

Trimmings
12 eyelets and an eyelet machine
1 pair of black shoe laces
1 m (40 in) piped satin bias binding
1 jogging shoes label
40 cm (16 in) black ric-rac braid

Thread
blue, yellow, beige, black and white sewing machine thread

Instructions
Enlarge the pattern overleaf. Prepare vilene-backed shapes for machine appliqué and pin them in position on the background. Tuck the ric-rac and bias binding in place and tack. Tack the large shapes and glue the small pieces in position and then machine satin-stitch. When stitching the piped areas use a zipper foot. The suede shapes can be straight stitched because the fabric does not unravel. Stitch in the label and punch eyelets for the laces.

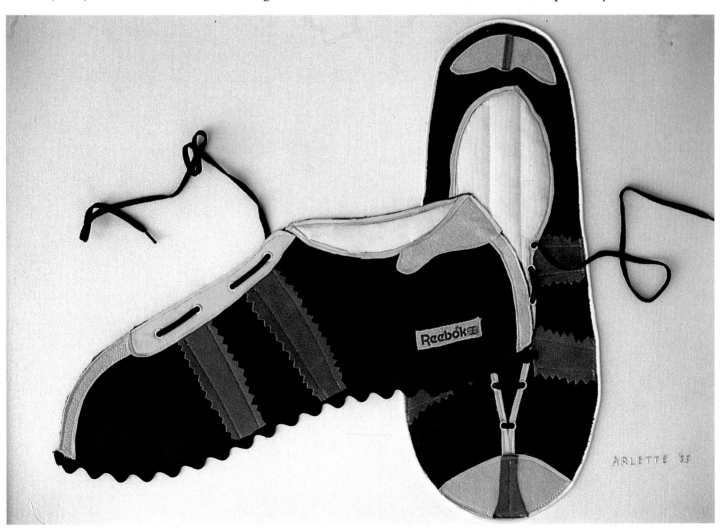

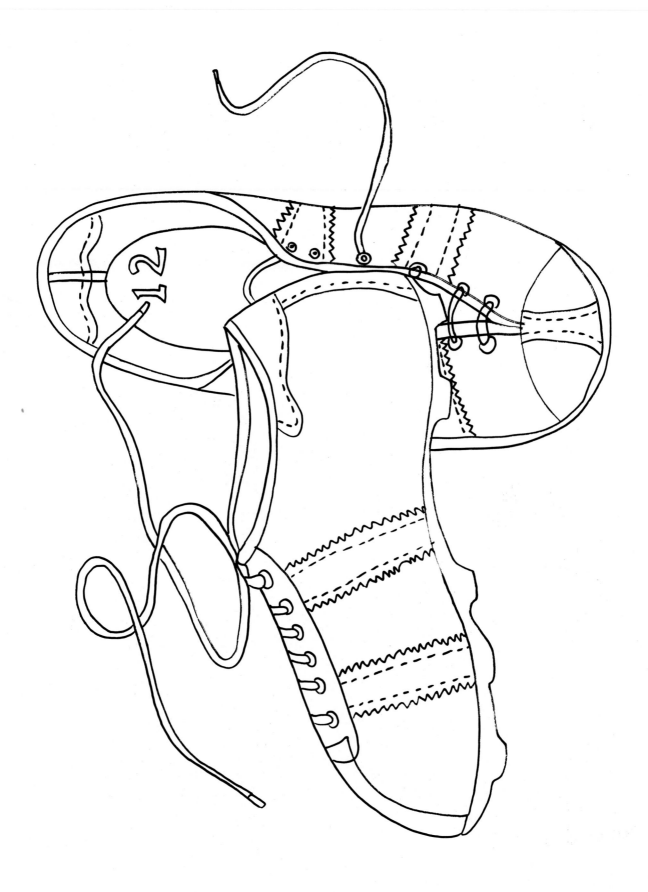

Party time

(Soda, cone and cake)

Ice cream colours give these designs instant appeal. These pictures are also lovely for a family room or even a cake and coffee shop.

Materials

Fabric

1.5 m (2 yds) white chintz for the background
50 cm (20 in) turquoise chintz for the details
30 cm (10 in) yellow, pink and green chintz for the details
a scrap of red chintz for the cherries
1 m (1 yd) iron-on vilene interfacing

Thread

red, green, turquoise, pink and white machine thread

Trimmings

10 round red buttons for the cherries on the cake
a small packet of transparent sequins and crystal beads for the bubbles

Instructions

Cut the white chintz into three 50 cm (20 inch) pieces. Enlarge the designs overleaf. Prepare the shapes for machine appliqué, assemble on the background and satin-stitch in matching thread. Attach sequins with tiny beads for the bubbles in the soda. Sew buttons onto the piece of cake for the cherries.

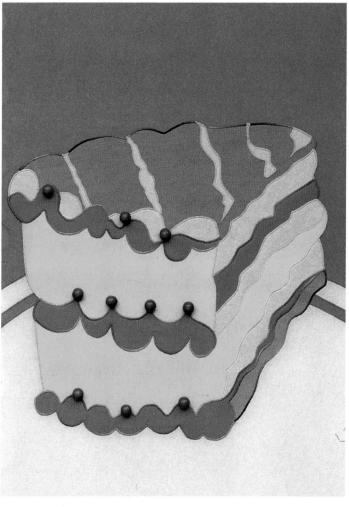

Appliqué tops

These are just a few ideas for designs that can be appliquéd to tops and T-shirts to 'jazz' them up. The flower would also look lovely on a handbag or on dinner mats. Geometric designs using semi-circles, cut-out triangles and diamonds are made in the same way.

Materials

Fabric
30 cm (10 in) black chintz for the large petals
a small piece of yellow chintz for the flower centres
scraps of pale green chintz for the leaves
50 cm (20 in) iron-on vilene interfacing

Thread
black, yellow and green machine thread

Trimmings
a packet of shocking pink sequins
a packet of tiny yellow seed beads

Instructions

This flower is made using the double vilene technique. Enlarge the design onto vilene, shiny-side upwards. Do not forget to include an underlap seam allowance on one edge where two raw edges meet. Prepare the shapes. Assemble and tack the leaves to the petals and position the centre. Place the tacked flower on a second, larger piece of iron-on vilene shiny side down. Satin-stitch around the design. Now bead the centre. Attach the shocking pink sequins and tiny yellow seed beads. Trim away the excess vilene. Repeat the basic flowers for as many images as you require. Hand hem the appliquéd motifs in place on the background with tiny blind hem-stitches.

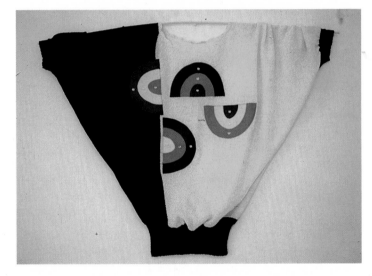

Tulips

Tulips in a row make an excellent headboard. They would also look stunning on the border of a tablecloth.

Materials

Fabric
cream polyester-cotton for the background (the quantity will depend on the width of the bed)
30 cm (10 in) of shades of pink chintz for the flowers
30 cm (10 in) of shades of green chintz for the leaves
1 m (1 yd) iron-on vilene interfacing

Thread
green and pink machine thread

Instructions
Enlarge the designs. Prepare the shapes using the double vilene technique and machine satin-stitch in matching colours. Cut away excess vilene. Make as many tulips as you require. Attach them to the background by straight stitching just inside the satin-stitch edge. The headboard can be framed or softly padded and hung like a wall hanging.

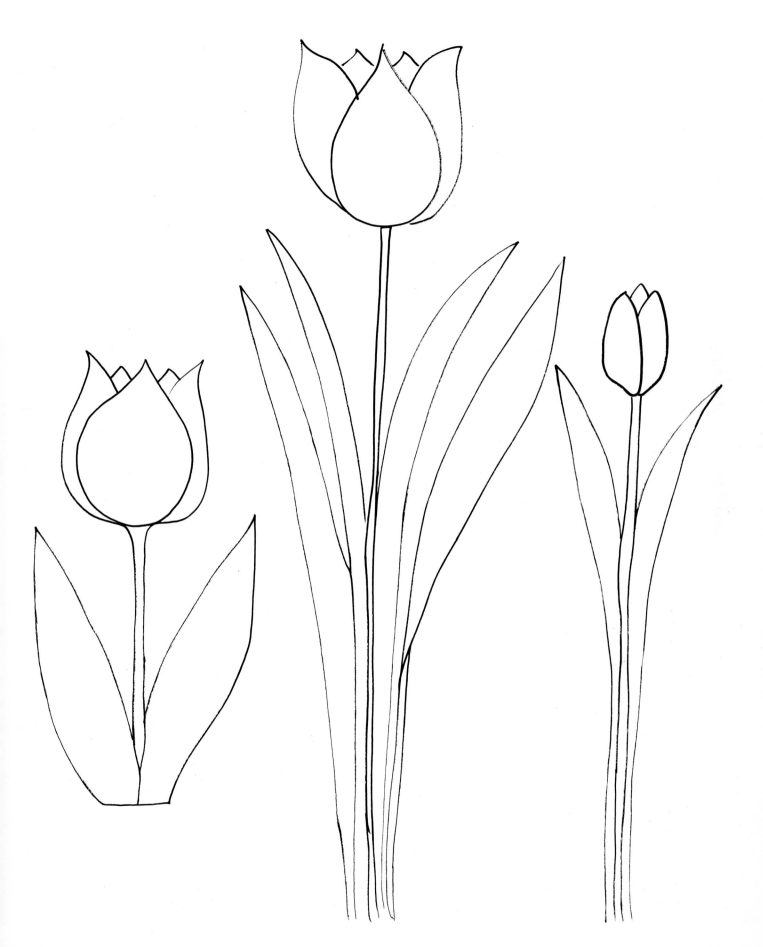

Country cousins

Make these charming little people and frame them yourself. These designs are suitable for machine or hand appliqué. Special effects are achieved by using gathered broderie-anglaise lace on the apron and pantaloons.

Materials

Fabric
50 cm (20 in) calico for the background
30 cm (10 in) granny print cotton for the dress and shirt
15 cm (5 in) blue cotton for the boy's trousers
small scraps of pink linen for the girl's hat
beige linen for the boy's hat
broderie-anglaise for the apron
brown cotton for the hair
rust cotton for the shoes
cream lawn for the face and hands
tiny bits of cream, white and blue cotton for the doll
1 m (1 yd) iron-on vilene interfacing

Thread
pink, green, white, brown, blue and cream machine thread
pink and green embroidery cotton for the rosebuds on the hat and the grass
two shades of beige embroidery cotton for the boy's basket
white and blue embroidery cotton for the doll's face and buttons

Trimmings
3 small pearl buttons for the shoes
1 m (40 in) narrow white broderie-anglaise for the apron trim and pantaloons

For two frames
2 × 36 cm (14 in) quilting hoops or rings
4 m (4 yds) broderie-anglaise lace
1 m (40 in) velvet ribbon for the bows
1 small tin of paint
1 bottle cold wood glue

Instructions

Trace the designs opposite and overleaf onto the iron-on vilene and prepare the shapes for machine appliqué. Satin-stitch the shapes in place on the background using matching thread. The apron skirt does not require vilene. Make a paper pattern by tracing the curve but make the top of the skirt twice the width of the yoke to allow for gathering. To attach the lace to the curved edge of the skirt, fold the edge of the skirt fabric under and top-stitch it to the lace. Gather the top edge of the skirt and tuck it under the yoke. Machine satin-stitch in place. Using the photograph as a guide, make two little lace frills for the pantaloons. Turn the side edges under and straight stitch. Cut a long strip of granny print (about 2 × 30 cm) (¾ × 12 inches) for the dress frill. Gather it and tuck under the dress. Satin-stitch the frill in position. Attach three buttons to the shoe and make bullion rosebuds and lazy-daisy leaves on the front of the hat. The girl appliqué is now ready for framing. Make the little boy figure in the same way as the girl.

To make a frilled hoop frame, paint the outer ring a suitable colour. Stretch the appliquéd picture between the rings. Trim away excess fabric but leave a small allowance and glue it to the inside of the frame. Gather the lace frill and glue in place with a wood glue. Tie a velvet ribbon through the adjustment screw to camouflage it. The picture is ready for hanging.

Two geese

This design is delightful for a baby's nursery or a really beautiful kitchen. The theme of the geese can be extended onto cot bumpers, cushions and duvet covers. In the kitchen, pot holders, place mats and gadget covers can be made to match.

Materials
Twin needle for the sewing machine

Fabric
80 cm (30 in) yellow plissé chintz for the background
50 cm (20 in) white chintz for the geese and wings
a small piece of polyester wadding for under the wings
30 cm (10 in) anglaise lace for one wing
50 cm (20 in) iron-on vilene interfacing

Thread
white machine thread
ginger embroidery thread

Trimmings
1 m (40 in) of white ribbon for the bows
1 m (40 in) of white anglaise lace for under the wing
2 tiny pearl beads for the eyes

Instructions
Enlarge the design overleaf. Trace the wings separately, cut them out and iron one vilene shape onto the anglaise fabric and one onto the white chintz. Decorate the chintz wing with twin needle machine stitching. Double vilene the wing outlines, machine satin-stitch around the edges and cut away excess vilene. Now prepare the shapes for the bodies and attach to the background. Machine appliqué the edges in white and use the looping foot for the chest fluff. Cut wadding the size of the wings. Hand hem the wings in position with the wadding underneath each wing. Gather the anglaise lace and whip-stitch it to the underside of the wing. Trace the beak, eyes and webbed feet onto the iron-on vilene, shiny side down. Cut out the vilene shapes and iron into position on the background ready for embroidery. Make a spider's web for the eye and top with the pearl bead. The feet and legs are a combination of bullion, satin- and chain-stitch. The beaks are embroidered in Romanian stitch. Make bows and attach them to the geese with a few backstitches.

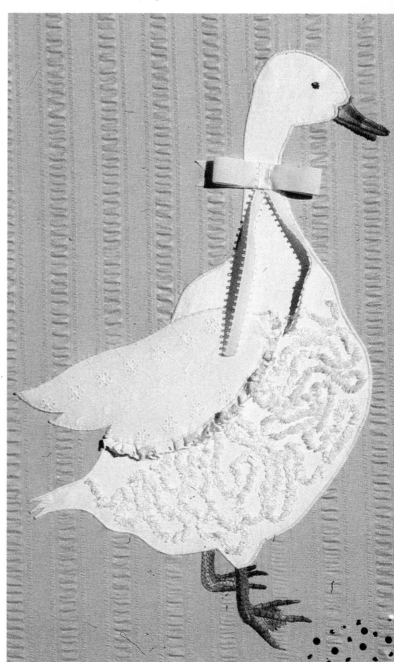

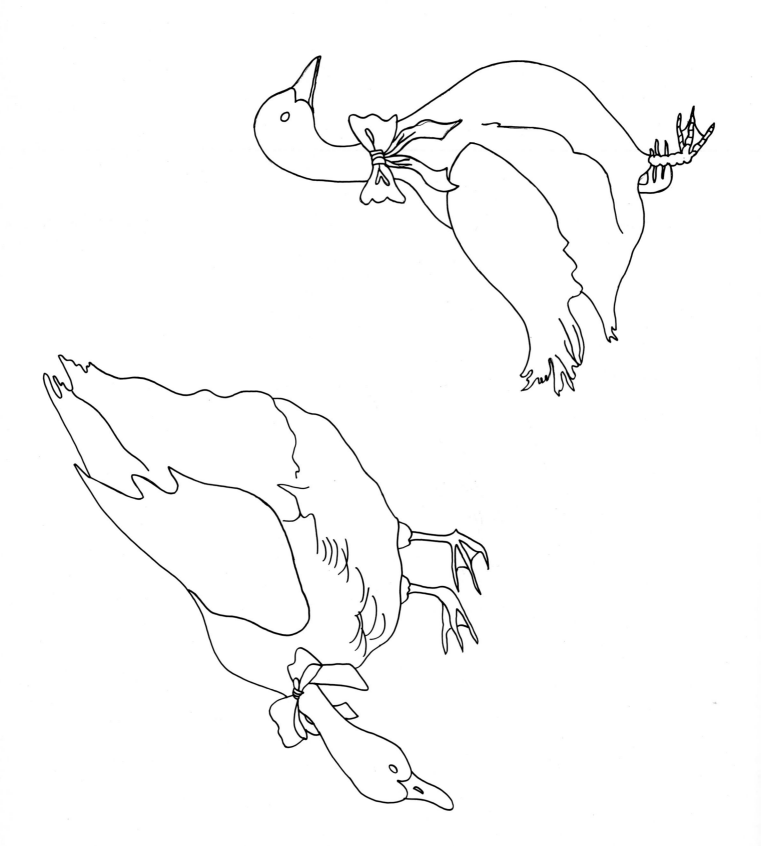

Landscape

The shades of blue and beige and the tree reflections in the appliqué landscape give a feeling of peace and tranquillity.

Materials
Twin needle for the machine

Fabric
50 cm (20 in) pale grey cotton for the sky
50 cm (20 in) cornflower-blue cotton for the water
50 cm (20 in) dark beige cotton for the beach
30 cm (10 in) light beige cotton for the distant beach
30 cm (10 in) light blue cotton for the water
50 cm (20 in) white cotton for the water's edge
30 cm (10 in) brown cotton for the tree trunks
a small piece of rust cotton for the rock

Thread
matching machine thread

Instructions
Enlarge the design. Prepare the shapes for machine appliqué and assemble on the background. Satin-stitch in corresponding colours. Twin needle the water's edge.

Gymnasts

These pictures are a perfect example of balance and design. The rhythm is emphasized by linear embroidery. These designs can be reduced and appliquéd onto tog bags.

Materials – *little gymnast*

Fabric
50 cm (20 in) beige cotton for the background
50 cm (20 in) pale blue T-shirt cotton for the leotard
small scraps of blue suede for the shoes
50 cm (20 in) cream cotton for the body
1 m (1 yd) iron-on vilene

Thread
matching machine thread
caramel and plum embroidery thread

Instructions
Enlarge the design overleaf. Prepare the shapes for machine appliqué. Assemble on the background and satin-stitch in place in corresponding colours. Draw the leotard patterns and embroider with raised chain in plum thread. Chain-stitch the hair in varying directions to suggest the pigtail. Make a bullion chain for the hair elastic.

Materials – *male gymnast*
Looping foot for the sewing machine

Fabric
80 cm (30 in) brown cotton for the background
50 cm (20 in) cream cotton for the body
50 cm (20 in) white cotton for the gym clothes
30 cm (10 in) rust cotton for the rings
scraps of white towelling for wrist bands
1 m (1 yd) iron-on vilene interfacing

Thread
white, brown, cream and rust machine thread
cream and brown embroidery thread
metallic silver thread for the chains

Instructions
Enlarge the design. Prepare the fabric shapes for machine appliqué and assemble on the background. Machine satin-stitch in place referring to the photograph for thread colours. Fill the hair with looping foot stitches. Embroider the chain using four strands of cream thread in rows of raised chain. The metallic links are a combination of buttonhole stitch, bullions and satin-stitch in silver thread.

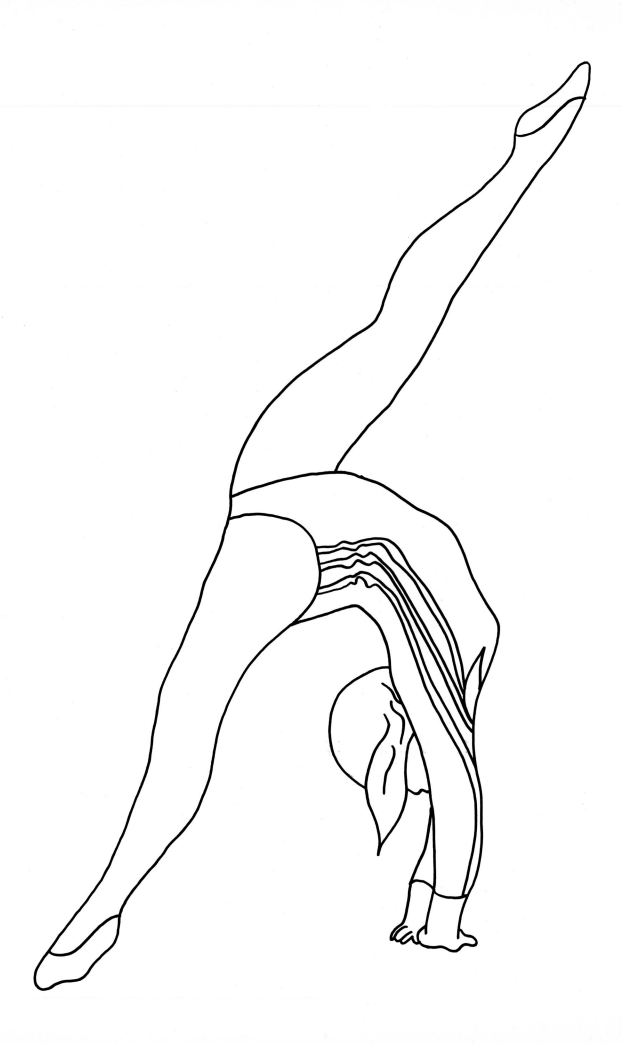

Palms on the beach

A special effect fabric gives this design an exotic feel. To make a very long wall panel or for use as a headboard for a double bed, extend the design by moving the palms.

Materials

Fabric

50 cm (20 in) grey linen for the sky
1 m (40 in) shaded moiré cotton for the water
30 cm (10 in) mustard chintz for the beach
30 cm (10 in) green silk for the grass
30 cm (10 in) green linen for the palm leaves
30 cm (10 in) white chintz for the clouds
a small strip of tan plissé chintz for the palm stems
a scrap of pink cotton for the sun
a small piece of beige, light-weight wool for the island
50 cm (20 in) iron-on vilene interfacing

Thread

white, green and tan embroidery cotton
cream, green, tan, beige, grey, pink and white sewing machine thread

Instructions

Enlarge the design overleaf. Cut a piece of the sky fabric, 100 × 40 cm (40 × 15 inches) and a piece of the water fabric 100 × 20 cm (40 × 8 inches). With right sides facing, sew the two fabrics together. Press the seam open. Prepare the pieces for the clouds, island, sun, beach and grass and assemble them on the background fabric. Machine satin-stitch them in place. Now use the double vilene technique for the large palms. Cut away excess vilene and position the palms on the background. Using the blind hem-stitch, hand hem them in place. This technique gives the palms a raised effect. Trace the boats and small palms on vilene with the shiny side down. Cut out the shapes and iron them onto the background. Embroider over the vilene – satin-stitch in green for the flags, chain-stitch in white for the sails and satin-stitch in rust for the boat hulls. Use cream bullion rosebuds for the coconuts, green Romanian stitch for the palm leaves and rust satin-stitch for the stems. Draw the flying birds onto the background and hand embroider with white chain-stitch.

Bags galore

With two basic bag patterns, some photographs for ideas and creative imagination, a wonderful bag collection can be yours.

Materials – pansy satchel

Fabric
50 cm (½ yd) feather leather, hessian or chintz in a suitable colour
50 cm (½ yd) cotton lining in matching or contrasting colour
small pieces of light and dark beige suede for pansies
small pieces of iron-on vilene interfacing

Thread
beige machine thread

Trimmings
a 15 cm (6 in) zip
small red and bronze beads
short gold bugle beads

Instructions

Trace the pansies directly onto the vilene. Using the double vilene technique, prepare, assemble and satin-stitch the design. Bead the centre, crusting in bronze beads, outlining in bugles and creating the dangles by starting with one bugle and one small red bead and slowly increasing the number of bugle beads to five.

Enlarge the bag pattern overleaf. Cut two pieces of feather leather and one of lining for the base, gusset and flap top. Stay-stitch the lining to the matching leather piece. Join the gusset to the bag base pieces, right sides together. Turn to the right side and top-stitch. Fold the feather leather over the lining at the opening and top-stitch. Insert the zip into one side of the flap top.

Zigzag stitch the appliquéd and beaded pansies onto the other flap top. Join the two flaps, right sides together, leaving the top open. Turn through and top-stitch. Fold the top edge under and stitch the flap to the base on one side through all the layers. Make two narrow loops of leather 12 cm (5 inches) long. Stitch the loops onto the base, front and back, each side of the top flap. Cut a leather strap 6 × 80 cm (2½ × 31½ inches). Fold the sides to the middle and top-stitch. Attach to the loops.

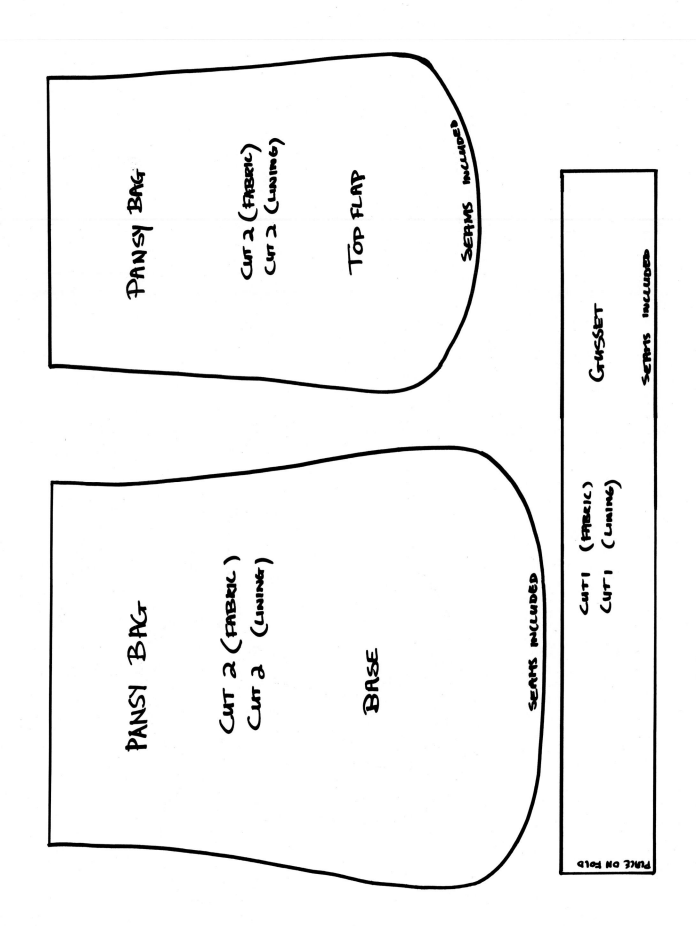

PANSY BAG

Cut 2 (FABRIC)
Cut 2 (LINING)

TOP FLAP

SEAMS INCLUDED

PANSY BAG

Cut 2 (FABRIC)
Cut 2 (LINING)

BASE

SEAMS INCLUDED

GUSSET

SEAMS INCLUDED

Cut 1 (FABRIC)
Cut 1 (LINING)

PLACE ON FOLD

Materials– round poppy bag

Looping foot for the sewing machine

Fabric

50 cm (½ yd) hessian, chintz or feather leather
50 cm (½ yd) cotton lining in matching or contrasting colour
red and green suede for poppies and for cord channel
small pieces of iron-on vilene interfacing

Thread

red, green and black machine thread

Trimmings

2 m (2 yds) draw string

Instructions

Cut from both hessian and lining one 35 × 80 cm (14 × 31½ inch) length for sides, one circle 23 cm (9 inches) in diameter for the base, and one strap 6 × 80 cm (2½ × 31½ inches).

Prepare the appliqué. Trace the poppies directly onto the iron-on vilene. Cut out and iron the vilene shapes onto red suede for the flowers and green suede for the stems, buds and centres. Machine satin-stitch the green centres on the flowers and then make the loops in black thread with the machine looping foot. Now position the poppies on the hessian rectangle keeping the lining separate. Machine satin-stitch the poppies onto the bag at the petal divisions only. Straight stitch the stems and buds in place. Join the short sides of the rectangle, right sides together, to form a cylinder. Pleat the cylinder to fit the base and stitch them together, right sides facing. Make the lining in the same way, slip it into the bag, wrong sides together, and catch the two bases together with a few backstitches. Fold the top edges in and top-stitch.

Cut two pieces of red suede 3 × 38 cm (1¼ × 15 inches). Attach the suede strips 3 cm (1¼ inches) down from the top edge along each side of the bag, leaving the ends open. Join the strap and its lining, right sides together, and pull through. Sew the strap inside the bag on opposite sides. Cut the draw string cord into two pieces. Using a safety pin, thread the cord through the suede band. Begin at one side, thread right round the bag and exit on the same side with one piece. Begin at the opposite side with the other piece of cord. Knot the ends together and pull up.

This bag lends itself to any decoration – abstract, floral, geometric, ribbon weave, beading or buttons.

Two little mice

Two sweet little mice to frame and hang as miniatures. The patterns can be traced directly or enlarged. The designs are suitable for hand or machine appliqué or even just embroidery. The procedure for making the little mouse with the parcel is described below. Make the mouse with the flowers in the same way.

Materials

Fabric
a scrap of sprigged cotton for the dress
a scrap of beige linen for the apron
a tiny piece of plaid for the parcel
30 cm (10 in) cream linen for the background
30 cm (10 in) iron-on vilene

Thread
rust, black, green and gold embroidery thread
nylon invisible thread for the whiskers

Instructions

Trace the design onto the iron-on vilene, shiny side down. Prepare vilene-backed shapes for the bonnet, dress, apron and parcel. Assemble the design directly onto the background and tack in position. Trace the face, hands and tail onto the iron-on vilene, shiny side down. Cut out and iron the vilene pieces in place on the background. Machine satin-stitch the clothes and then hand embroider the details. The face and tail are split-stitch, the eyes are bullion rosebuds, the hands and fingers are split-stitch and bullions and the grass is stem-stitch. Make a gold thread bow and stitch it onto the parcel. The whiskers are invisible nylon thread blackened with fabric paint.

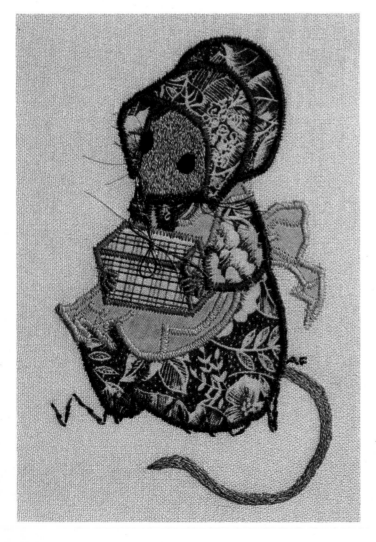

Yemenite lady

Adapted from an Israeli craft poster, this design takes full advantage of appliqué, beading and embroidery.

Materials

Fabric
50 cm (20 in) black cotton for the background
50 cm (20 in) shocking pink chintz for the top
30 cm (10 in) green, purple and blue chintz
30 cm (10 in) gold lamé for the scarf
30 cm (10 in) cream cotton for the face and arms
50 cm (20 in) iron-on vilene interfacing

Thread
matching machine thread
black, light brown, white and red embroidery thread

Trimmings
1 m (1 yd) exotic braid for the neck band
a selection of beads and sequins in all colours and sizes
50 cm (20 in) wide ribbon in black, white, shocking pink and gold
pink fabric paint

Instructions
Enlarge the design. Prepare all the flat appliqué shapes for machine appliqué and assemble on the background. Machine satin-stitch in corresponding colours. Hand embroider the face in satin-stitch and chain. Plait the ribbons and hand hem the plait to the turban and the waist band. Machine stitch the braid onto the neck line of the top. Using beads and sequins, make necklaces and bracelets (see p65). Use beads for earrings and shawl tassels. Pink in the cheeks with fabric paint.

Geranium skirt

Take a plain white skirt and top and add a few appliqué geraniums – it will look like a designer's creation.

Materials

Fabric
50 cm (20 in) each of purple, lilac, yellow and green chintz
1 m (1 yd) iron-on vilene interfacing

Thread
matching machine thread
embroidery thread in purple, lilac, yellow and green

Instructions

Enlarge the design. Trace a selection of flowers and leaves onto your iron-on vilene. (The number of flowers will depend on the width of the skirt.) Iron the cut vilene shapes onto the back of various fabrics. Cut out the flowers and leaves. Position each vilene-backed shape onto the back of a larger piece of corresponding fabric. Machine satin-stitch the details and edges of each shape in matching thread. Now you have a selection of overlocked, double-faced fabric motifs. Embroider the centres of the flowers with contrasting colours in french knots and bullions. Make green rosebuds in the centre of the leaves. Arrange the designs around the hem and machine satin-stitch over the edges of the appliqué where they join each other and the skirt upper edge. (Open the zigzag setting if the machine tends to bunch.) Cut the excess skirt fabric away at the back.

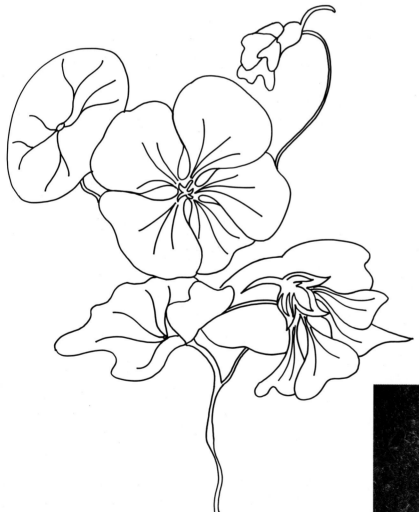

150

Butterfly lampshade

Liven up an old lampshade by making 3D butterflies for it.

Materials

Fabric
30 cm (10 in) cream anglaise fabric
30 cm (10 in) iron-on vilene interfacing

Thread
cream machine thread

Trimmings
2 m (2 yds) 3 mm (⅛ in) wide ribbon for the feelers
a small quantity of polyester wadding for the butterfly abdomens

Instructions

Trace the design onto the iron-on vilene. Cut out the shape and iron onto the back of the anglaise. Cut out the vilene-backed shape. Place this shape onto a larger piece of anglaise fabric, wrong sides together. Machine satin-stitch the two layers of fabric together leaving a small opening for the feelers and the stuffing. Push a little wadding into the abdominal cavity. Make a curved shape for the feelers using the ribbon. Slip the raw ends into the opening and close the abdomen. Cut away the excess fabric and the butterflies are ready to be stitched onto the lampshade.

Karate hold-all

This is a picture with the added dimension of handy pockets.

Materials

Fabric
80 cm (30 in) black cotton for the background
30 cm (10 in) each of white and red cotton
50 cm (20 in) iron-on vilene interfacing
tiny scraps of grey cotton

Thread
black, white and red machine thread

Trimmings
5 m (5½ yds) of red, piped bias binding
1 small gilt chain
a karate badge

Instructions

Enlarge the designs. Cut the background 50 × 93 cm (20 × 37 inches). Cut one double pocket 33 × 39 cm (13 × 16 inches) and four double pockets 20 cm (8 inches) square. Prepare the shapes for machine appliqué and assemble each design onto one side of each pocket. Machine satin-stitch. Catch the chain in place with a few backstitches and hem the badge in position. Sew the piped bias binding onto the pocket edge using a zip foot. With right sides together, join the pocket lining to the appliquéd tops leaving a small opening. Trim seams, clip curves and turn through. Straight stitch the pockets in place leaving the top edges open.

Orchids

Suede provides the perfect foil for the glitter of beads and together they reveal the exotic essence of the orchid. This design can be made as a picture, or individual orchids can be used on glamorous clothing.

Materials

Fabric
small pieces of suede in shades of blue, plum and beige for the flowers and avocado and bottle green for the stems and buds
80 cm (30 in) beige linen for the background
50 cm (20 in) iron-on vilene interfacing

Thread
machine thread in blue, beige, plum and green

Trimmings
a selection of sequins, large and small, in plum, blue, white and pink
bugle beads and small beads in gold, white pearl, blue and plum

Instructions

Enlarge the design. Be sure that your colours balance in each group of orchids. Prepare vilene-backed shapes for machine appliqué. At this point continue with the double-vilene technique in preparation for bead and sequin embellishment, or leave the shapes as they are with raw edges because the suede does not unravel.

Bead the individual flowers using the photograph as your guide. Feel free to enjoy the potential the beads offer. A few suggestions for the beading: work the lines with couching or flat sequining to emphasize direction; work the centres with clusters and even free dangles to give a third dimension.

When all the flowers are beaded, assemble them paying special attention to the negative spaces. If the shapes are already overlocked, hand hem the flowers in position and open zigzag the stems. If the shapes are raw edges, machine satin-stitch the orchids and zigzag the stems and buds.

Rugby players

This picture is the companion piece to the games and sport quilt. The vibrant colours are the most important aspect of this design.

Materials

Fabric
50 cm (20 in) turquoise poplin for the background
30 cm (10 in) each of black, white, light and dark blue, red, pink, apricot, yellow, green and cream poplin
a small piece of rust suede for the rugby balls
1 m (1 yd) iron-on vilene interfacing

Thread
matching machine thread in black, white, blue, red, pink, yellow and cream
apricot, blue and pink embroidery thread

Trimmings
2.5 m (2½ yds) navy ribbon for the bench strips
50 cm (20 in) polyester wadding for padding the chests and rugby balls

Instructions
Enlarge the design. Prepare all the fabric pieces for each rugby player for machine appliqué and assemble on the background fabric. Before tacking, cut the wadding for the chests and rugby balls using the fabric pieces as a template. Tack the wadding to the wrong side of the chest fabric and machine quilt on with diamonds, one with squares and another in vertical strips. It is easier to embroider the numbers at this point. With a pencil draw the number onto the fabric and embroider in continuous chain. Now tack all the pieces in position, tucking the ribbon strips under the legs. Machine satin-stitch in the colours shown in the photograph.

B.M.X. bike

Fun decor for any bike enthusiast's bedroom. Machine appliquéd, and hand-finished with embroidery and fancy trimmings.

Materials

Fabric
1 metre (1 yd) of cream corduroy for the background
1 metre (1 yd) of red cotton for wheels, handlebars and crossframe
50 cm (20 in) of black cotton for the rest of the frame
50 cm (20 in) of grey cotton for the wheel rims, pedals and the small details
a small piece of brown suede, or imitation suede, for the saddle
1 metre (1 yd) of iron-on vilene interfacing

Trimmings
3 metres (3 yds) silver ric-rac for the chain
4 metres (4 yds) silver cord (soutache) for the wheel spokes
3 metres (3 yds) of wide, red ric-rac for the tyre treads

Thread
red, black, green and brown machine thread. Silver embroidery thread

Instructions

Enlarge the bike pattern to full size. Trace, cut and prepare all the bike parts and assemble the design, referring to the photograph, onto the background for direct machine appliqué. Tack all the large pieces tucking the red braid half way under the wheel rims to give the tread. The small pieces can be glued using a glue stick and then machine satin stitched. Alternatively use the double vilene technique. Then machine the whole bike to the background using open zig-zag or straight stitch. The bike chain is two rows of silver ric-rac and the spokes are silver soutache. Hand embroider the details: french knots on the handlebars, rosebuds and spider's web for the bolts and screws and satin stitch for the lettering.

Big bonnets

Adapted from wrapping paper, these little figures are a lovely combination of patterned and plain fabric, a real 'mix and match'.

Materials
Looping foot for the sewing machine

Fabric
1 m (1 yd) white cotton for the background
50 cm (20 in) cotton fabric in sprigs, spots and plains in pink, green and plum for the bonnets, dresses and aprons
30 cm (10 in) cream cotton for the faces, hands and ankles
30 cm (10 in) white anglaise fabric for the blouse, pantaloons and flowers
1 m (1 yd) iron-on vilene interfacing

Thread
matching machine thread
green, black, white, pink, brown and beige embroidery thread
variegated brown machine thread for the hair

Trimmings
2 m (2 yds) plum, narrow ribbon
2 m (2 yds) pink, narrow ribbon
4 plum buttons for the dress back and one small plum button for the earring
pink fabric paint

Instructions
Cut the background fabric in half. Enlarge the designs opposite and overleaf. Refer to the photographs and choose your fabric and the suitable threads. Prepare the pieces for machine appliqué and assemble them on the backgrounds. Machine satin-stitch the edges and fabric details. Make looping foot (see p72) hair on one figure and machine embroidered hair on the other. Hand embroider the facial details in a combination of chain and satin-stitch. Make bows and decorate with the ribbon. Paint the cheeks pink.

Oriental fantasy

This is a soft quilted wall hanging which combines appliqué, patchwork, embroidery and beading.

Materials

Fabric
1.3 m (1½ yds) beige cotton for the background squares
4 m (4½ yds) green poplin for the lining and border
2 m (2½ yds) brown poplin for the diamond border
50 cm (20 in) each of green, turquoise, purple, blue, pink, yellow and plum cotton for the creatures and the diamonds
40 cm (16 in) salmon satin for the fish
a small piece white moiré taffeta
2 m (2 yds) iron-on vilene interfacing
polyester wadding for quilting

Thread
a selection of machine threads in red, green, yellow, blue, salmon and beige
pink, turquoise, blue, yellow, purple, red, green embroidery thread

Trimmings
16 little brass bells for the corners
a selection of small and large sequins
50 cm (20 in) gold ric-rac braid
50 cm (20 in) silver ric-rac braid

Instructions

Cut the beige fabric into four 60 cm (24 inch) squares and add a 6 mm (¼ inch) seam allowance. Enlarge the appliqué designs on the following pages and, using the photograph as a guide to colour combinations, prepare the shapes for machine appliqué. Assemble each creature on a beige background. Machine satin-stitch the owl in place with green thread, the peacock with blue, the butterfly with red and the fish with salmon. Hand embroider the details referring to the enlarged photographs. The eyes are spider's web, groups of stars are on the chests and herringbone is used on the outlines. Use sequins and braid for the wings, feathers and scales.

Cut out 81 7 cm (2¾ inch) vilene squares and iron them onto a mixed selection of the fabrics used in the appliqué.

Cut strips of brown fabric for the borders:

3 strips – 130 × 10 cm (52 × 4 in)		Add 6 mm (¼
2 strips – 150 × 10 cm (60 × 4 in)		inch) seam
2 strips – 60 × 10 cm (24 × 4 in)		allowance all
		round

Join the peacock to the fish and the owl to the butterfly with short brown strips. Machine satin-stitch six diamonds onto each strip with yellow thread. Join the two pairs of appliqué squares to the sides of a brown centre strip 130 × 10 cm (52 × 4 inches). Appliqué 13 diamonds to this strip. Attach the two 130 × 10 cm (52 × 4 inches) side strips and appliqué 13 diamonds onto each. Now sew the remaining two brown strips onto the top and bottom of the hanging and appliqué 15 diamonds in place on each strip. Cut the polyester wadding 5 cm (2 inches) larger than the finished top. Tack and quilt around the beige squares. Cut the green lining in half crosswise and stitch the two halves together side by side. Lay the lining on a flat surface and place the appliquéd top over it. Cut the lining so that 6 cm (2½ inches) extends beyond the polyester wadding. Wrap the green lining over the extra polyester wadding, turn under a small seam allowance and pin the lining onto the brown border edge. Machine through all the layers with an open zigzag in green thread. Sew the brass bells through all the layers at the corners of each square.

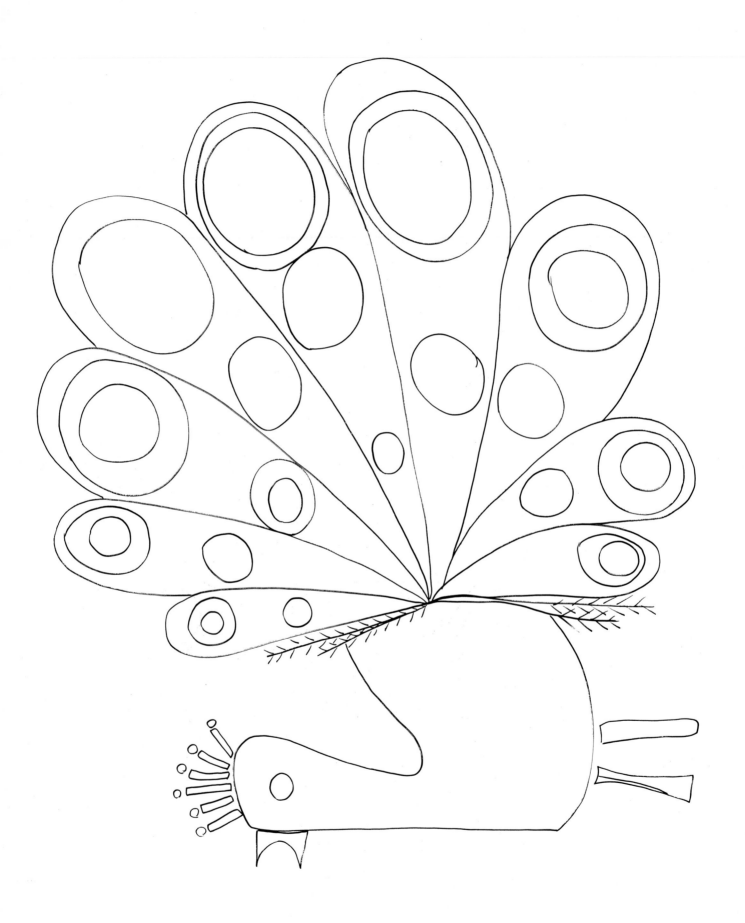

Beach cottages

This dynamic design is entirely machine appliquéd except for a few french knot waves. Depth is achieved through the diminishing sizes of the houses and not through colour change. If the picture looks too elaborate, create a smaller or less complex design using a few of the houses or even one on its own.

Materials
Twin needle for the sewing machine

Fabric
80 cm (30 in) cream calico for the background
50 cm (20 in) dark grey linen for the roofs
30 cm (10 in) pale grey linen for the side roofs
30 cm (10 in) dark brown and rust cotton for the doors and boats
30 cm (10 in) dark olive green cotton/linen for the windows
50 cm (20 in) olive green cotton/linen for the bushes
30 cm (10 in) dark blue cotton for the sea
30 cm (10 in) pale blue cotton for the sky
50 cm (20 in) beige cotton for the house shadows

Thread
brown, olive green, light and dark blue and grey machine thread
pale blue and white embroidery cotton

Instructions
Enlarge the design overleaf and transfer it to your background fabric. Prepare and cut out the contrast colour shapes using the photograph as your guide. Remember, superimposed pieces do not require seam allowances but where the raw edges of two pieces meet,

one edge must have an under-lap allowance. Pin and tack all the shapes in position on the background fabric. Machine appliqué the contrast shapes with self-coloured thread. All the linear detail on the houses and steps must be machine satin-stitched on a narrow, close setting using brown sheen. Twin-needle, in grey thread, the four most important rooftops. Suggest waves in the sea with a few swells of french knots.

Sports basket

Patchwork and appliqué sports equipment are all in one basket! This project is a marvellous way of using odd trimmings that have been cluttering the needle-work basket. The impact of the appliqué comes from the dominant use of primary colours.

Materials

Fabric

1.5 m (60 in) light blue poplin for the background
1 m (40 in) bright blue poplin for the basket
30 cm (10 in) white cotton for the tennis racquet and ping-pong balls
30 cm (10 in) red feather leather for the boxing glove
30 cm (10 in) navy blue cotton for the beach bat
30 cm (10 in) caramel corduroy for the rugby ball
30 cm (10 in) green spotted cotton for the tennis box
30 cm (10 in) yellow cotton for the quoit and tennis balls
scraps of brightly coloured cotton for the patchwork football
small bits of fabric for the skipping rope, spinning-top and shuttlecock
2 m (2 yds) iron-on vilene interfacing

Thread

black, white, brown, red, light and dark blue, yellow machine thread
white and red embroidery thread

Trimmings

1 white shoe lace for the boxing glove
1 brown shoe lace for the rugby ball
eyelets and eyelet machine
1 m (40 in) white twisted cord for the skipping rope
a piece of string for the tennis balls
30 cm (10 in) mesh for the tennis racquet
2 m (2 yds) white satin ribbon for the beach bat
50 cm (20 in) red ric-rac for the beach bat
a piece of wadding for the rugby glove

Instructions

Enlarge the design overleaf. Prepare all the shapes except the hexagon soccer ball, skipping rope and boxing glove, and tack them to the background. Machine satin-stitch using contrast and matching thread according to the picture. Using the hexagon pattern provided on page 77, create your patchwork soccer ball. Cut a circle 31 cm (12 inches) in diameter from the hexagon patchwork and appliqué it in position. Prepare the boxing glove using the double-vilene technique. Make the eyelets and thread the lace. Cut a piece of wadding the same shape as the glove and attach the glove with the wadding underneath using a blind hem-stitch.

Couch (see p72) the skipping rope in place. Double-vilene the handles, tuck a little stuffing under them and blind hem in place. Decorate the beach bat with ribbon and ric-rac. Embroider the tennis racquet and the tennis ball box details referring to the photograph. Make the eyelets and thread the shoe lace into the rugby ball. The feathers on the shuttlecock are done with a machine disc. (Use fly-stitch for hand embroidery.) Details on the tennis balls are created by open zigzag over a piece of string.

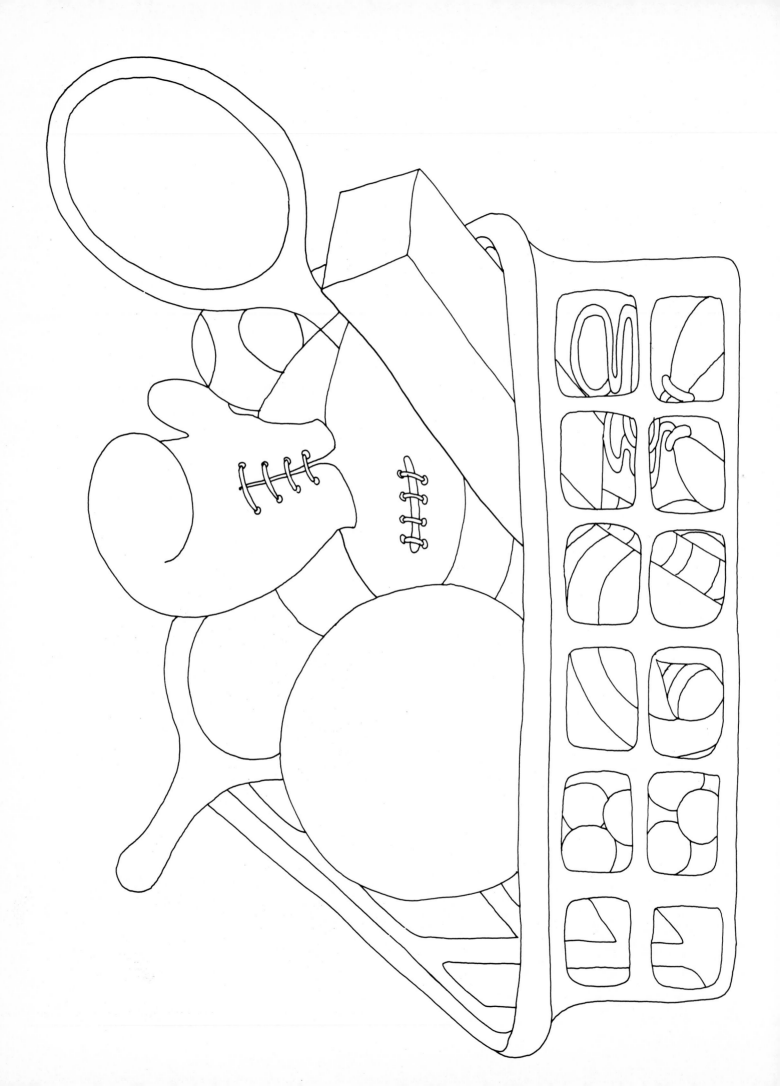

The enchanted garden

This is an advanced piece with a lot of embroidery. The design grows out of the background. There is a wonderful play of negative and positive shapes created by appliqué pieces and embroidered details.

Materials
Twin needle for the sewing machine·

Fabric
1 m (40 in) avocado green fine cotton for the background
50 cm (20 in) grey-green silk for the house
50 cm (20 in) dark green chintz for the bushes and windows
30 cm (10 in) rust chintz for the pathway
tiny pieces of terra-cotta cotton for the flower pot
small pieces of antique lace for the curtains
2 m (2 yds) iron-on vilene interfacing

Thread
various shades of green and rust machine thread
a multi-coloured selection of embroidery threads for the flowers and trees

Instructions
Enlarge the design overleaf. Trace the entire design onto the vilene, shiny side upwards. Iron the vilene onto one large piece of avocado green background fabric. Hold the fabric up to a window and draw all the embroidery details onto the front using a soft pencil. Prepare the shapes for the house, pathway, windows, flower pot, bushes and forest and tack them in place on the background. Machine satin-stitch the house, including the roof-tiles and steps, in a dark green thread. Satin-stitch the bushes, flower pot and pathway with matching thread. Twin-needle the brick pattern on the path. Hand hem small pieces of antique lace into the windows. Some areas of this design, such as the tree and daisy outlines, can be machine embroidered. If your machine has fancy stitches that look like stems or leaves, use them for some of the bushes. This is a design which allows appliqué artists to develop and explore their embroidery skills. Use the detail photograph. The giant chrysanthemums are raised chain, ordinary chain and bullion rosebuds; the spiky flowers are two-coloured pekinese stitch; the hollyhocks are continuous chain; the small flowers are mixtures of lazy daisy, spider's web, french knots, buttonhole wheels, woven circles, rosebuds and stabstitch; the tree trunks are split-stitch; and the leaves are closed or open Romanian stitch.

Violet seller

Grey and burgundy hues make this olde world picture ideal for the living room or bedroom. Buttons and bows, tassels and silver mesh, all add to the quiet charm.

Materials

Fabric
80 cm (30 in) grey, flocked satin for the background
50 cm (20 in) silver mesh for the shawl and gloves
50 cm (20 in) burgundy velveteen for the jacket and hat
50 cm (20 in) granny-print brushed cotton for the dress
30 cm (10 in) cream lawn for the face and hands
30 cm (10 in) caramel chintz for the hair
30 cm (10 in) hessian for the basket
30 cm (10 in) pink-slub brushed cotton for the scarf
2 m (2 yds) iron-on vilene interfacing

Trimmings
4 exotic buttons for the cuffs
2 small pink buttons for the dress
50 cm (20 in) silver tassel/fringing
50 cm (20 in) narrow burgundy ribbon
30 cm (10 in) 12 mm (½ in)-wide grey satin ribbon

Thread
grey, burgundy, cream, caramel and pink machine thread
burgundy, grey, bottle-green, blue, black, cream and caramel embroidery cotton

Instructions

Enlarge the design overleaf. Prepare the shapes for the face and hair using the double vilene technique. Machine appliqué face and hair outlines. Now decorate the hair using the looping foot on your machine. Embroider the facial features using tiny backstitches for the nose and eye outlines, satin-stitch for the mouth, eyes and eyelids and chain-stitch for the eye-brows. Prepare the remaining shapes and assemble them on the background. Fit the face and hair into the design. Machine satin-stitch around all the shapes except the face and hair. Use an open zig-zag to attach the face and hair because the edges are already overlocked. Make small bows and attach these to the hat with a few invisible stitches. Add fringing, ribbon and buttons. Finally hand embroider the violets. The petals are satin stitch, the centres french knots and the leaves Romanian stitch.

Dream machine

This appliqué is advanced because the shapes are complex and abstract and the illustration is even more detailed than the photograph. This project should present a challenge for the adventurous appliqué artist.

Materials

Fabric
1 m (40 in) light grey polyester/cotton for the background
50 cm (20 in) each white and black chintz for bike details
30 cm (10 in) red chintz for bike details
30 cm (10 in) metallic synthetic leather
30 cm (10 in) beige chintz for the rims
scraps of open-weave, orange wool for the reflectors
a piece of transparent self-adhesive plastic for the visor
50 cm (20 in) of iron-on vilene (if using the double vilene technique)

Thread
black, white, red and beige machine thread
red, black and orange embroidery cotton
metallic silver thread for the screws and bolts

Instructions
Enlarge the design overleaf. Simplify the details if it is too elaborate. Work closely with the photograph, numbering shapes that are repeated or similar. Make a tracing which you can place over the design to help you assemble the parts correctly. Prepare the large pieces first. Tack them in place on the background. Prepare the small shapes, glue them to the background with a stationery glue stick and then machine satin-stitch. An alternative method for the small shapes is to prepare them using the double-vilene technique and then hand hem them in position. Any shape which is too difficult to manipulate in the machine can be hand embroidered instead. The self-adhesive plastic for the visor must be appliquéd in conjunction with the fabric. The details can be embroidered in a variety of different stitches. Nuts and bolts look great in silver spider's web and bullion knots. The design must develop as you go along. Let creativity take control and enjoy it.

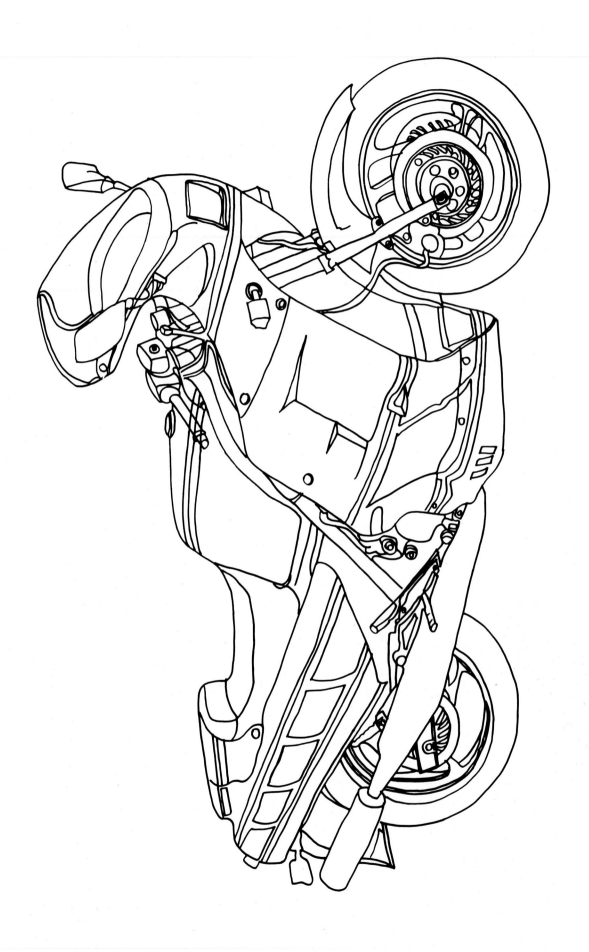

Trapunto cushion or quilt

Cream on cream is the concept behind this design. Start with one block and make a cushion. Then create a quilt to match.

Materials

Fabric
for cushion
50 cm (20 in) cream polyester-cotton lawn or cotton for the quilted cover
50 cm (20 in) muslin
50 cm (20 in) calico for the cushion
a piece of polyester wadding 40 cm × 40 cm (15¾ × 15¾ in)
a small bag of polyester stuffing for the cushion

for quilt
(The measurements and quantities are for a 137 cm (4 ft 6 in) double bed)

4 m (4½ yds) cream polyester-cotton lawn or cotton for the quilt top
4 m (4½ yds) cream dacron, lawn or cotton for the ruffle
4 m (4½ yds) muslin
4 m (4½ yds) calico
a large cream sheet 160 × 240 cm (64 × 95 in) for the lining
24 squares of polyester batting 40 × 40 cm (16 × 16 in)

Thread
cream waxed quilting thread
cream machine thread

Trimmings
20 m (21½ yds) gathered cream lace (for the quilt)
2 m (2 yds) gathered cream lace (for the cushion)

Instructions

for the cushion

Cut a piece of background fabric 40 cm (16 inches) square and a corresponding piece of muslin. Tack the muslin to the wrong side of the top fabric. Enlarge the design below. Mark the quilting pattern on the fabric, using an erasable marking pen, dressmaker's pencil or a very light lead pencil. Make tiny running stitches following the outlines of the trapunto motif (the flower) using the waxed quilting thread. When the flower is complete, make small slits in the muslin and insert the stuffing into the cavity of each petal. Close the slit with tiny whip-stitches. Cut a piece of wadding and calico lining the same size as the background fabric. Sandwich the wadding between the top layers and the lining. Tack. Quilt through all the layers using tiny running stitches and moving from the trapunto outwards.

Cut another piece of cream fabric 40 cm (16 inches) square for the back of the cushion. At this point a ruffle, lace or piping can be attached. With right sides together, sew around the cushion, leaving a small opening for the cushion. Trim seams, clip corners and turn.

For the cushion, cut two pieces of calico 40 cm (16 inches) square and seam them together leaving a small opening. Clip the corners and turn through. Stuff until plump and whip-stitch the opening closed. Insert the cushion into the cover and close with tiny whip-stitches.

for the quilt

Cut 24 squares each of cream top fabric, muslin and wadding 40 cm (16 inches) square. Make 12 quilted trapunto squares as described for the cushion. Mark the other 12 squares for diamond quilting only (no trapunto flower). Join four squares together in a strip alternating trapunto and plain. Continue joining sets of four squares until you have six strips. Sew two strips together, right sides facing. Press the seam open and flat, and sew the lace over the seam. Continue joining the strips and adding the lace. Once all the strips are connected (four squares across by six squares down) attach the three central vertical rows of lace but not the outer edge lace.

For the ruffle, cut the balance of cream fabric into long lengths, 40 cm (16 inches) wide. If the bed has a toe (footboard), the strips must be hemmed and gathered in three separate ruffles. If not, the ruffle can be stitched together in one long length, hemmed and gathered. Pin, tack and sew the ruffle onto three sides of the quilt top. Right sides together, sew the lining to the top on three sides leaving the top open. Trim seams, clip corners and turn through. Turn under and slip-stitch or machine stitch the top closed. Finish off by sewing the lace onto the border edges of the quilt.

Rose balloon basket

This is a most beautiful appliqué picture adapted from a painting by Wilma Langhamer.

Materials

Fabric

80 cm (30 in) variegated blue satin for the background
50 cm (20 in) pink satin for the roses
30 cm (10 in) green moiré taffeta for the hills
30 cm (10 in) blue moiré taffeta for the mountains
30 cm (10 in) olive green organza for the leaves
a selection of cream and pink scraps for the houses and the people
1 m (1 yd) iron-on vilene interfacing

Thread

matching machine threads
shades of green, pink, cream and brown embroidery thread
silver metallic thread for the telescope

Trimmings

2 m (2 yd) olive green soutache for cords
pink fabric paint

Instructions

Enlarge the designs overleaf. Trace all the appliqué pieces for the mountains, hills and little houses onto the vilene and prepare the shapes for appliqué. Attach the hills to the mountains and the houses to the hills using matching thread. Embroider the forest and bushes using clusters of french knots and bullion rosebuds.

Machine satin-stitch the mountains onto the background. Prepare a selection of roses for appliqué using the double vilene technique. Machine satin-stitch around these roses with pink thread. Trim away excess vilene and hand embroider the details with french knots, bullion rosebuds and stem-stitch referring to the detail photographs. For the stuffed and quilted petals see p48 on stuffed shapes. Hand hem the stuffed petals to the matching roses. Now make a number of green organza leaves referring to p42 for the technique. Assemble the prepared roses and leaves on the background and hand hem in place. Prepare for machine appliqué the two figures and the inside of the basket, assemble them on the background and machine satin-stitch in place in matching colours. Trace the basket front onto your vilene, shiny side down. Cut out and iron onto the background. Hand embroider the basket in alternating satin-stitch blocks, one horizontal and then one vertical, in different shades of green. French knot the man's hair and make a plait for the woman by satin-stitching the crown of the head and leaving lengths of thread at the nape of the neck which can be plaited. Satin-stitch a silver telescope. French knot tiny eyes and shade the cheeks with pink fabric paint. Position the soutache cords. Chain-stitch in green around the basket edge, catching both cords simultaneously. Attach the top of the cords with a few backstitches under the leaves and petals.

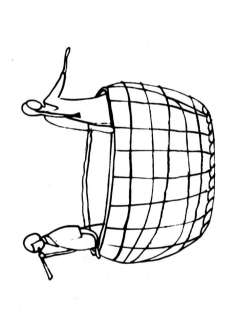
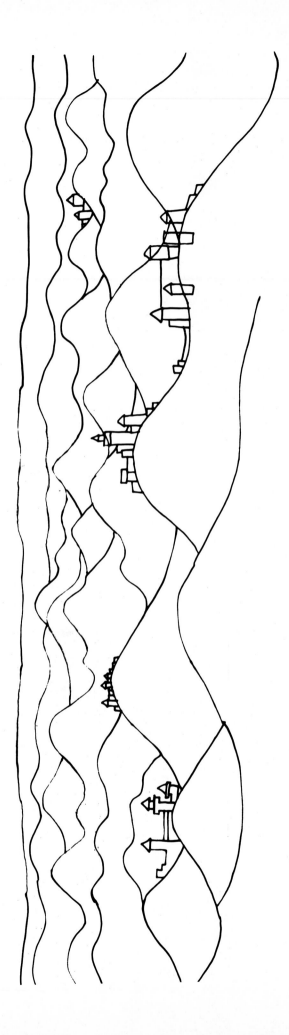

Games and sports quilt

This quilt spells FUN. It is made with a mixture of appliqué, patchwork, embroidery and quilting.

Materials

Fabric

5 m (6 yds) navy blue polyester-cotton for the background
50 cm (20 inches) pieces of cotton in a selection of plain colours for all the objects
a piece of tapestry weave for the tennis racquet
a small piece of paisley fabric for the king of hearts and the snakes
polyester wadding for the quilt (the quantity will depend on the width)

a navy blue flat sheet for the lining
2 m (2 yds) iron-on vilene interfacing

Thread

sewing machine thread in matching colours
embroidery thread in white, black, yellow, green and red

Trimmings

3 shoe laces and eyelets for the roller skate, football boot and boxing glove
scraps of ric-rac braid for skittles
a piece of string for the tennis balls
11 m (12 yds) of ready piped turquoise bias binding

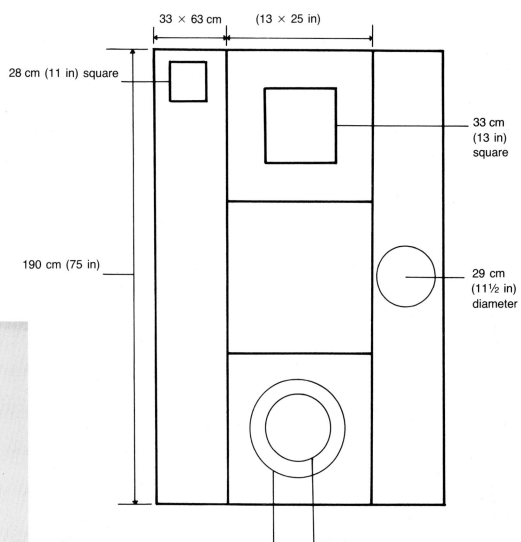

33 × 63 cm   (13 × 25 in)

28 cm (11 in) square

33 cm
(13 in)
square

190 cm (75 in)

29 cm
(11½ in)
diameter

33 cm (13 in) diameter

45.5 cm (18 in) diameter

Instructions

Using the sketch as a guide, mark three 63 cm (25 inch) squares and two 33 × 190 cm (13 × 75 inch) side pieces on the background fabric. Add 12 mm (½ inch) seam allowance and cut out.

The football, dart board, chess board and backgammon are all patchwork. Use the templates provided and refer to the illustration for sizes. (For techniques see pp 77-79).

Enlarge the design for the appliqué pieces. Prepare the rest of the objects for machine appliqué and assemble on the background fabric. Machine satin-stitch the tennis equipment onto the central square; the chess set onto the top square and the dart board onto the lower square. Referring to the photograph, position the other equipment and machine satin-stitch onto the side panels. Sew all the embroidery details, add the braid and make eyelets for the shoe laces.

Cut the polyester wadding the size of each panel. Tack the wadding to the wrong side of each panel and quilt around the appliqués in a navy blue straight stitch.

Using a zip foot, machine stitch the turquoise piped binding to the top and bottom of the tennis panel. Now join the chess board and dart board to the tennis panel. Sew the binding onto both long sides of the centre panel. With right sides facing, sew the side panels to the main panel. Attach the piping all round the quilt border. Cut the navy blue sheet to the size of the quilt top. Right sides together, machine all round leaving a small opening. Turn through and slip-stitch the opening closed. The lining can be further secured with a few backstitches at the junction of the panels.

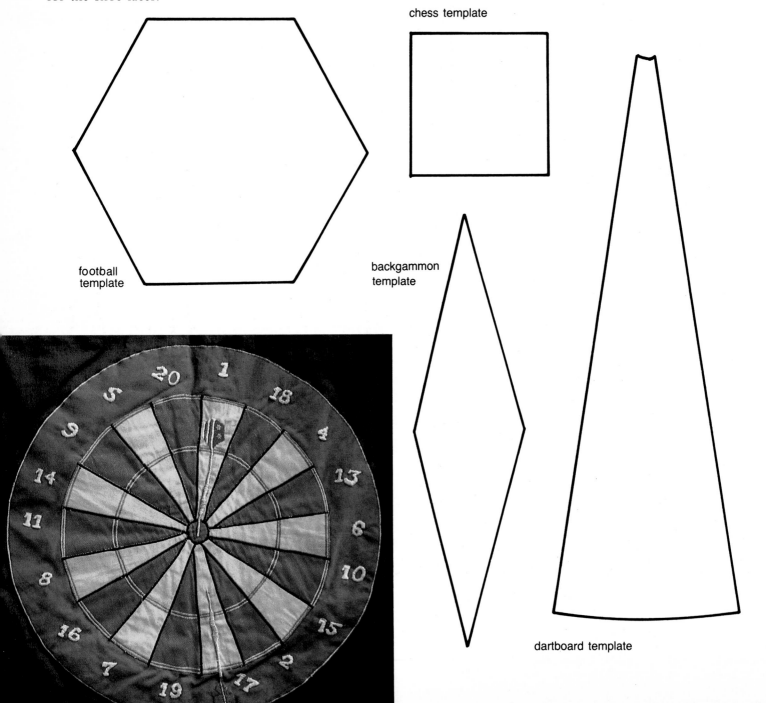

football template

chess template

backgammon template

dartboard template

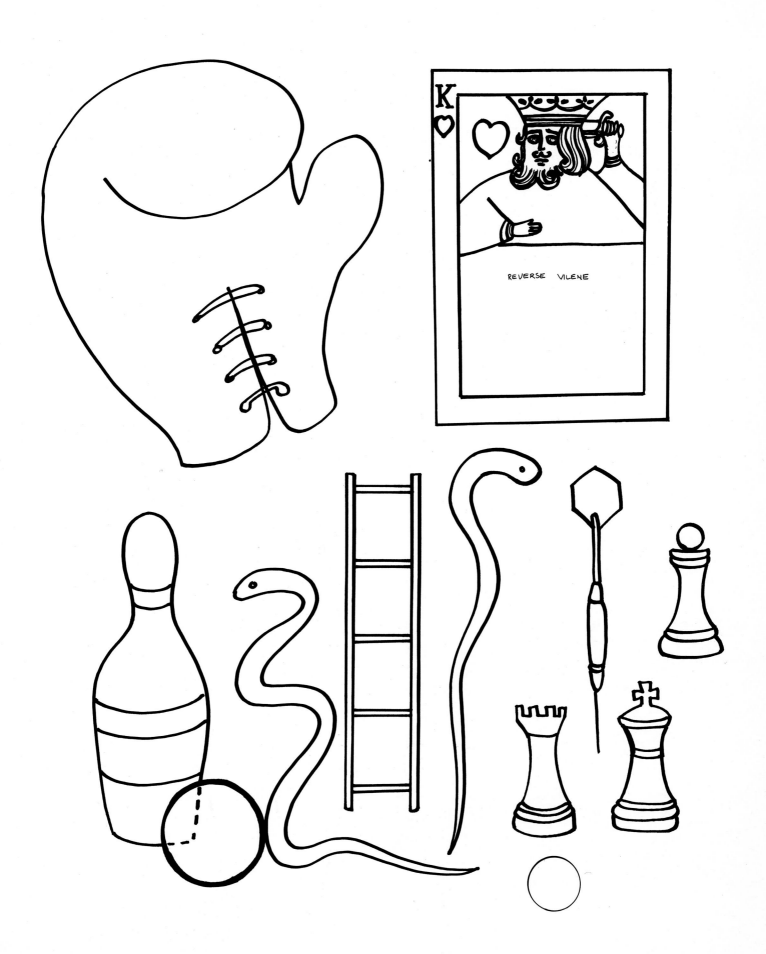

REVERSE VILENE